Weddings

For All Seasons

Published by

**krause
publications**

700 East State Street • Iola, WI 54990-0001
715/445-2214 • FAX: 715/445-4087   www.krause.com

Please call or write for our free catalog of publications. Our toll-free number to
place an order or obtain a free catalog is 800-258-0929 or please use our regular
business telephone 715-445-2214.

Library of Congress Catalog Number 2001088102
ISBN 0-87349-283-8

Acknowledgments

There are numerous people who helped make this book of wedding ideas a
special one. A huge "thank you" to the designers who offered their terrific ideas—
Kim Wakefield, Lisa Vollrath, Bucky Farnor, Kari Lee of The Leather Factory,
Christine Beyer, Sherry Bartman, Carolyn Vosburg Hall, Jane Davis, Betty Auth,
and Blanch Lind—not to mention the manufacturers who generously gave of their
resources and talents—Hot Off The Press and Wilton Industries. And, it is necessary to also acknowledge graphic artist Kim Schierl for her outstanding work and
photographers Ross Hubbard, Kris Kandler, and Bob Best for their creativity and
patience.

Welcome to Weddings For All Seasons

This book was created with *you* in mind, the bride-to-be. We all know that planning for the big day, from the major decisions of the date and where to hold the reception to minute details like choosing the perfect place cards, can be exhausting. And that's why we've made it easy for you to shop for and assemble all of the projects—whether they are quick and easy favors or elaborate centerpieces—in this book.

This book is meant to be a smorgasbord of ideas, with projects that appeal to all tastes and skills, not to mention budgets! To make it easy for you to coordinate all of the pieces for your wedding, from the ceremony to the reception, the projects are divided into six different categories, from the traditional crisp whites of summer to "general" projects that can be adapted for use throughout the year. (Note that even in these different categories, there are numerous styles to choose from; for instance, the Summer/Traditional grouping includes four different bridal bouquets, each of which uses a different array of flowers.) In an effort to make finding projects in the categories easier, each page has a colored bar running down its edge, from top to bottom. Further, the Index, on page 128, is organized by category.

COLOR KEY

	Spring
	Summer/Traditional
	Autumn
	Winter
	Callas
	Year 'Round

While we have arranged the projects according to a color scheme or seasonal theme, don't be locked into what the pictures show; feel free to make changes as desired, using different flowers or colors throughout the designs per your preference.

To make this book an all-in-one resource, we have included some basic instructions for creating wedding floral designs and making and decorating cakes. Because of space constraints, we were not able to include every aspect of these topics, but your local library and bookstore are full of excellent resources.

Finally, information about wedding customs and traditions throughout the world are also included in this book. While some couples prefer to infuse their wedding day with personal touches, many choose to rely on traditions, from the bride wearing a white dress to the tossing of the bridal bouquet and garter.

In the end, never forget that this is your day, and it can be as simple or elaborate and traditional or modern as you desire. Regardless what you choose, make it a day to remember!

Congratulations and Enjoy!

Amy Tincher-Durik
Weddings For All Seasons Coordinator

Table of Contents

Basic Techniques

Florals • 6
Cakes • 11

Chapter 1
The Shower • 14

Whimsical Favors and Photo Album • 16
Hat Place Card • 17
Tiered Ivy Bowl Centerpiece • 17
Whimsical Centerpiece • 18
Bottle Centerpiece • 19
Roses and Hearts Shower Cake • 20

Chapter 2
The Bridal Party • 22

Callas and Satin Arm Sheaf • 24
Callas and Berries Arm Sheaf • 26
Callas and Berries Nosegay • 28
Callas Boutonniere • 30
Callas-trimmed Bag • 30
Callas and Pearl Comb • 31
Lily and Hydrangea Nosegay • 32
Hand-wrapped Bouquet • 34
Periwinkle Scabiosa Cone • 36
Satin Flower Girl Basket • 38
Lily Corsage • 40
Hydrangea Boutonniere • 40
Ribbon and Hydrangea-trimmed Veil • 41
Ribbon and Rose Hair Bow • 42
Rosebud Ring Pillow • 43
Rose Arm Sheaf • 44
Gardenia and Ribbon Bouquet • 46
Orchid Cascade Bouquet • 48
Mixed Cascade Bouquet • 50
Single Orchid Corsage • 52

Double Orchid Corsage • 52
Triple Rose Corsage • 53
Single Rosebud Boutonniere • 53
Pearl and Satin Veil • 54
Pearl and Satin Comb • 55
Trimmed Ring Pillow • 56
Bridal Garters • 57
Raffia-wrapped Bouquet • 58
Cascading Bouquet • 60
Attendant's Basket • 62
Gardenia and Rose Bouquet • 64
Red Rose Bouquet • 66
Red Rose Clutch • 67
Ribbon and Rose Ball • 68
Rosebud Halo • 69
Suede Jewelry Pouch • 70
Bead Strung Jewelry Set • 72

Chapter 3
The Ceremony • 74

Unity Candle Holder • 76
Heart Pew Bow • 77
Unity Candle Set • 78
Garden Altar Arrangement • 80
Ranunculus Pew Bow • 82
Braided Pew Bow • 83
Fall Harvest Altar Arrangement • 84
Layered Invitation • 86
Perfect Programs • 87

Chapter 4
The Reception • 88

Callas and Glass Centerpiece • 90
Callas Place Card Frame • 92
Callas Candle Holder • 92
Callas Favors • 93
Arched Centerpiece • 94
Pastel Topiary • 96
Favor Boxes • 98
Bubble Favors • 99
Cone Topiary • 100
Wedding Ring Centerpiece • 102
Swan Favors • 104
Bag Favor • 105
Box Favors • 106
Slipper Favors • 107
Decorated Toast Glasses • 108
Decorated Guestbook Pen • 109
Daisy Cake • 110
Terra Cotta Centerpiece • 112
Favor Boxes • 114
Chair Garland • 115
Rose Ivy Bowl • 116
Rose Place Card Holder • 117
Cherub Place Cards • 118
Wedding Bell Favors • 119

Chapter 5
After the Big Day • 120

Callas Frame • 122
Photo Album Cover • 124
Shadow Box • 125
Winter Wedding Scrapbook Page • 126
Our Wedding Day Scrapbook Page • 126
Thank You Card • 127

Project Index by Theme • 128

Flowers have long been included in wedding ceremonies, because they symbolize such things as fertility, purity, new life, and never-ending love. But, now many brides choose flowers based on their preference, the flowers' colors, and the time of year during which they are getting married, not necessarily symbolism.

The wonderful thing about silk flowers is they will look amazing—no wilting or drooping—for the duration of your wedding day. Years ago, most brides preferred fresh flowers because silk flowers looked too artificial, but that is no longer the case! You may be surprised by how life-like many silks look.

This section includes some basic techniques to guide you through the process of creating floral designs for your wedding, even if you have little or no experience working with silk flowers. All you need are some basic tools and supplies, shown below, and an assortment of flowers!

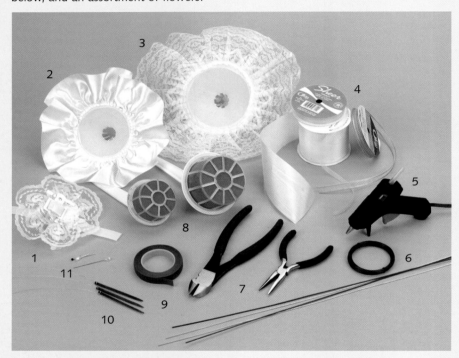

1. Velcro Corsage Wristlet. 2. Small satin collar. 3. Large lace collar.
4. Various widths and colors of ribbon. 5. Hot glue gun and glue sticks.
6. Wire in various gauges. 7. Wire snips.
8. Bouquet holders. 9. Floral tape. 10. Wired floral picks. 11. Pearl-head pins.

DESIGNING BASICS

While it would be impossible to teach you everything about wedding floral design in a few pages, the purpose here is to give you some information to start you in the right direction. Once you understand some basic terminology and design concepts, you should be able to apply them to all types of projects, including bouquets, corsages, and centerpieces.

Focal flowers are the foundation of each arrangement; these are the flowers that will draw the most attention. It is standard to use odd numbers of focal flowers in arrangements. **Line flowers** give an arrangement height and width and create a look of balance; often, they have buds on a tall stalk, like gladiolas and delphiniums. **Mass flowers** add fullness to an arrangement. They are usually round and are often referred to as face flowers; they have one flower per stem and provide the focal point of color. Roses, sunflowers, and carnations are all examples of mass flowers. **Fillers**, which can be both flowers and leaves, provide a finishing touch and a full feeling. They are usually small and have numerous buds per stem and give a smooth transition between mass flowers and line flowers. Some of the most-used fillers are baby's breath, eucalyptus, and ferns.

There are numerous design principles to keep in mind when you are working with florals, like balance, contrast, and rhythm. **Balance** refers to not only whether an arrangement looks like it is going to topple over but also how the individual parts of the design relate to one another. One way to add interest to a design is with **contrast**, both in the colors that are used and the "mix" of different flowers and foliage, some with contrasting textures. A design that has **rhythm** helps move the eye smoothly through it.

CASCADING BRIDAL BOUQUET

This traditional bouquet is a favorite among brides any time of the year. This pretty example features white and purple-tinted roses (the focal and mass flowers, respectively) along with small purple flowers, fillers, and longer lily-of-the-valley, line flowers, that create the main lines of the cascade.

1. First, start defining the shape of the bouquet with the focal flowers. Then, begin filling in the design with leaves.

2. Now insert the mass flowers.

3. To begin creating the cascade at the bottom of the bouquet, add the smaller filler flowers. Also use these flowers to fill in gaps in the design.

4. To complete the cascade, insert longer line flowers first to the bottom of the bouquet and then throughout the design.

The finished bouquet.

ROUND ATTENDANT'S BOUQUET

This bouquet is complementary to the Cascading Bridal Bouquet. While many of the same flowers in that design are used here, it is customary to not duplicate all of the flowers from the bride's bouquet in the attendants'. Here, the main focal flowers from the cascading bouquet—white roses—are omitted and the mass flowers—purple-tinted roses—are featured, and a new flower has been introduced: the daisy.

1. First, start defining the shape of the bouquet with the focal flowers. (**Note:** Unlike the Cascading Bridal Bouquet, here the leaves have been maintained on the roses; you can add additional foliage after the design is complete.)

2. Now insert the smaller fillers, using

Tip: If the smaller filler flowers' stems are limp, you may need to reinforce them with a wire pick. First, hold the pick against the stem and then wrap the wire around the stem to secure the two together. Next, cover the stem and pick with floral tape.

wire picks to support to the stems, if necessary.

3. To complete the design, insert the larger mass flowers. Fill in any gaps with leaves.

Some people begin their bouquets by outlining the shape with leaves. In our examples, we have started with the focal flowers and added leaves later to fill in the shape.

Regardless of how you start a bouquet, when designing it, imagine all of the stems meeting in one place in the bouquet holder's foam.

The finished bouquet.

THE HAND-WRAPPED BRIDAL BOUQUET

In recent years, hand-wrapped bouquets have gained popularity. This simple, yet striking, design is very easy to assemble. For this sample, four callas are shown as the focal flowers and three large roses are the mass flowers. **Note:** Many of the hand-wrapped bouquets included in this book do not show the ribbon wrapped along as much of the stems' lengths as shown here.

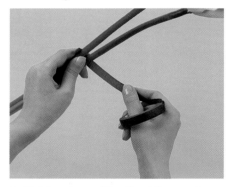

1. Holding two of the focal flowers in a staggered position, join them together, about 1 foot down the stems.

While few modern brides would include herbs in their bouquets, hundreds of years ago brides carried strong-smelling herbs and spices to frighten off evil spirits, bad luck, and illness.

2. **Optional:** Before you tape the first mass flower to the joined focal flowers, you may want to trim some of its lower leaves.

3. Now tape the mass flower to the focal flowers. Continue adding the focal and mass flowers, staggering their heights to create interest in the design.

4. When all of the flowers are joined, put a dab of hot glue at the point where the securing ribbon will be attached; this will be at approximately the same point where the floral tape begins.

5. For a finished look, fold over the edge of the ribbon about 1 inch. Secure the end of the ribbon to the dab of hot glue and begin wrapping the ribbon around the joined stems. Do not wrap ribbon around the entire length of the stems. **Note:** After the bouquet is finished, you can either leave the stems staggered at the bottom or cut them flush with heavy-duty wire snips.

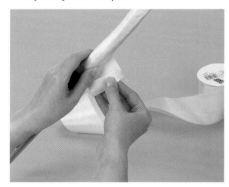

6. When you are done wrapping the ribbon around the stems, cut it and fold over the edge about 1 inch.

USING FLORAL TAPE

While holding the items to be tapped together in your left hand along with the start of the floral tape, hold the roll of tape with your right hand. Use tension as you pull the tape, which has a wax adhesive, off of the roll and twist the items to "wrap" them with tape.

7. Put a dab of hot glue at the point where the securing ribbon will be attached. Further secure with pearl-head pins.

The finished hand-wrapped bridal bouquet.

CORSAGE

There are two options for making a corsage: it can either be pinned onto the recipient's clothing (Option 1) or worn on the wrist (Option 2). In the samples shown, three roses, two white and one purple-tinted, are used as the focal flowers, and the small purple flowers seen in the both the Cascading Bridal Bouquet and Round Attendant's Bouquet are used sparingly to complete the design. The key to a great corsage is minimizing the bulk.

In order to get a more natural, realistic look to your silk flowers, feel free to manipulate the wires in the stems by bending and curving them.

Option 1

1. Using floral tape, join one focal flower to a bunch of filler flowers, adding support to the stems, if necessary. Repeat for the other two focal flowers.

2. Now add leaves behind the focal and filler flowers.

3. Using floral tape, join one of the focal flowers to the colored focal flower.

4. Tape a multi-loop bow to the two focal flowers that have been joined.

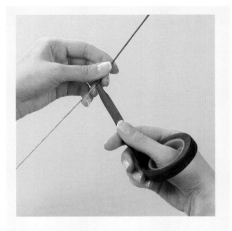

To make a simple bow to add to any corsage, bouquet, or other arrangement, first wrap a piece of 20 to 24 gauge wire with floral tape. (**Note:** While this looks "cleaner," some designers chose not to wrap the wire prior to using it.) Next, make loops with ribbon, twisting the ribbon where it is held in the right hand. Now insert the wrapped wire into the main loop. Fold the wire over the ribbon and twist, securing the bow.

9

5. Now take your final focal flower and tape it to the others, below the ribbon.

The finished corsage.

Option 2
To make a wrist corsage, follow Steps 1 through 4 of Option 1. In order to make this type of corsage, you will need a corsage wristlet.

CUTTING RIBBONS
Throughout this book, you will see instructions that say "angle off the ribbons ends" or "cut a 'V' in the ribbon ends"; both are ways of giving the ribbon a more finished look.

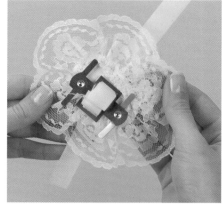

1. Attach the two joined focal flowers and ribbon from Step 4 to the wristlet by clamping them in one set of the metal prongs. **Hint:** Needle nose pliers may come in handy.

2. Take the final focal flower and turn it so that its stem is pointing toward the joined flowers on the wristlet. Attach this flower to the wristlet (under the two joined flowers) by clamping it in the remaining set of metal prongs. If the corsage does not feel secure, you can reinforce it by wrapping a piece of wire around all of the stems where they are joined and twisting the wire on the back.

The finished wrist corsage.

THE BASIC BOUTONNIERE
Absolutely anyone can make a boutonniere! All you need is one flower, for example one chosen from the bride's bouquet, some wire snips, and floral tape.

1. Using wire snips, cut the flower's stem, leaving about 3 inches.

2. Snip a set of leaves from the discarded stem. Using floral tape, attach the leaves to the flower.

hile making and decorating your own shower or wedding cake may seem like a daunting task, it can really be quite fun and easy. Like designing with florals, all you need are patience and practice—and some indispensable tools from Wilton Industries. (**Note:** The basic information presented here is by no means complete; consult any of Wilton's publications listed on page 13 for more complete instructions.)

First things first: A great cake starts with quality tools and supplies. Some of the basics you will need are shown here, but you may also find such items as cooling racks, colored foil to wrap cake boards, icing colors, and tip couplers helpful. Make sure you have all of the necessary tools and supplies ready before you begin.

1. Spatula. 2. Serrated knife. 3. Cake board with plastic dowel rods. 4. Cake pan.
5. Decorating bag. 6. Various tips. 7. Tip brush.
8. Wooden dowel rods (to be used in place of plastic variety).

BAKING

If you are baking your own cake, follow the recipe instructions for such things as recommended batter amounts and special directions for the pan size you are using. Prior to baking, grease the inside of the pan generously with vegetable shortening (not butter, margarine, or liquid vegetable oil) and sprinkle flour into the pan, shaking the pan so the bottom and all sides are covered. Pour out any excess flour.

After baking is complete, let the cake cool for about 10 minutes. Loosen the cake from the pan using a knife and unmold it by placing a cooling rack against the pan then turning both over; carefully lift the pan off. Let the cake cool for approximately 1 hour.

LEVELING

When the cake is completely cool, you will need to level it prior to filling the layers and/or icing. You can either place the cake on a cake board to do this or put it back in the baking pan to get a flush cut. Keeping the knife as level as possible, saw off the top of the cake. Wilton also produces a cake leveler that can be used instead of a knife.

FILLING THE LAYERS AND ICING THE CAKE

If you are making a layered cake, you will need to put icing between the layers. Using a decorating bag and large round tip (like tip 12), put a circle of icing just inside the edge of the cake (the side you leveled should be up). After you have completed the circle, fill in the middle area with icing, spreading it evenly with a spatula. Repeat for all layers.

When you are done filling the layers, you will need to ice the entire cake. To do this, put a large amount of icing in the center and spread it across the top, using the spatula. Smooth the top and work icing down the sides of the cake. Cover the sides with icing, smoothing it with the spatula and working one section at a time. Continue until you have iced all sides, smoothing the icing as you go. Let the icing sit for about 15 minutes before decorating or preparing a tiered cake for assembly.

DECORATING BAGS, TIPS, AND COUPLERS

Some of the most essential tools you will use to ice and decorate a cake are bags, tips, and couplers.

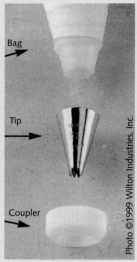

Bags and couplers: There are three different types of bags, each of which can be used depending upon your project or preference: feather-weight, disposable plastic, and parchment.

Each of these bags can be used with or without a coupler, which allows you to change tips quickly and easily—without changing the bag. To prepare the bag prior to using a coupler, you need to push the coupler into the bag, cut off the tip where the bottom screw thread is outlined against the bag, and push the coupler through the opening; then you can put on a tip and secure it with the coupler ring. To change tips, simply unscrew the current tip and replace it with another.

To fill the bag with icing: Hold the bag with one hand and fill it with about 1/2 cup of icing, using an angled spatula. Do not overfill the bag, because icing could come out the top! Twist the top portion of the bag in order to force the icing down.

Tips: Metal tips allow you to create countless designs and motifs with icing, from simple balls and rosettes to more advanced figures and flowers. There is a wide variety of tips available, including ones that are specially used for stars, leaves, roses, and ruffles. With proper care, tips should last a lifetime; store them upright on pegs to prevent them from being bent out of shape and wash them after each use with hot, soapy water (or use a tip brush, if necessary).

ASSEMBLY

In order to assemble a tiered cake, you will need supportive plastic or wooden dowel rods. The rods need to be placed in the bottom tier, in the area in which the upper tier will be placed. On the bottom cake, center a cake board the same size as the upper tier; press into the icing and remove. Insert a dowel rod into the cake, straight down, inside the area marked from the cake board. Mark the rod height, pull the rod out, and cut the necessary amount of rods to support the upper tier (the larger the tier, the more dowels you use). Insert the rods into the tier, pushing straight down, until they hit the board below. Repeat the process for all tiers.

PILLARS

Pillars are a popular way to add height and drama to a wedding cake. While the photo shows pillars being put into a base cake plate (along with a fountain, which is covered below), the principle is the same for whatever tier you are working with: make sure the feet of the cake plate, into which the pillars

will be inserted, are facing up. Put the pillars on the feet and carefully set the tier, which is also on a cake plate with the feet facing down, on the pillars. Continue adding tiers in this method.

Note: Assemble a cake on pillars at the reception site and take along extra icing, tips, etc. in case anything is damaged in transport.

Other Pillar Options

If you don't want to use traditional pillars to add height to a tiered cake, you can also use one or more champagne glasses. To add stability, use dowel rods in the tier below the glasses, as described above, and, using a hot glue gun, glue the glasses to the top of the "base" cake plate on which they will rest.

FOUNTAINS

Fountains are a beautiful way to add interest to a wedding cake display. They can be placed at the base of a cake, or at the top as a unique ornament. Assemble the fountain per the manufacturer's instructions and always test it to make sure it works properly.

One easy way to add pizzazz to a fountain is to color the water. While the fountain is running, add a couple drops of food coloring to the top portion, and voila!—now you have water that accentuates the cake's color scheme. If you are using the fountain at the cake's base, you can also arrange fresh or artificial flowers around it.

STAIRCASE

Staircases are an impressive addition to any tiered cake. Make sure the tiers joined by a staircase are an appropriate distance apart (if the staircase will not be joined by a bridge, allow 8" between the top and bottom, and 7" if it will be joined by a bridge). Adding a staircase is easy: arrange the main and "satellite" cakes in the approximate positions, gently insert the top of the staircase into the top side of the main cake, as shown, with the bottom resting on the satellite cake.

DECORATING

Wedding cakes are the perfect palette on which to create something your guests will never forget, whether it is done with the addition of "extras," like doves, flowers that coordinate with those used during the ceremony, pearls, and ribbon or with innovative decorating with frosting.

CAKE BOARDS

It is recommended to use cake boards that are 2" larger than the cake. To wrap a board, trace the board onto a wrap,

like Fanci-Foil Wrap, 3" or 4" larger than the board. Cut the Fanci-Foil along the outline, put the board on the foil, and cut slits in the foil, wrapping it around the board; tape the foil to the board to secure.

BUTTERCREAM ICING AND ROYAL ICING

Two of the most frequently used icings for wedding cakes are buttercream and royal. You can purchase a buttercream frosting mix (Wilton has a Creamy White Icing Mix that needs to be mixed with butter and milk).

To color icing, dip a toothpick in the color and swirl it into the icing, using a spatula to blend. Add color a little at a time, keep in mind that a small amount goes a long way—in buttercream frosting, the colors will intensify after 1 to 2 hours.

RESOURCES

Wilton Industries has created some amazing resources you are sure to find helpful, whether you are a novice or experienced cake maker or decorator.

Cake Decorating, 2001 Wilton Yearbook. Full of cake ideas, basic instructions, and shows the complete line of Wilton products.

Cake Decorating Beginner's Guide: Step-by-Step Instructions. Includes basic information and twelve birthday- and special occasion-themed cakes.

The Wilton School: Decorating Cakes, A Reference & Idea Book. The complete book of cake decorating, from techniques and borders to working with fondant and making flowers.

Wilton Bridal Showers. This book has eight themes for coordinating cakes, favors, and table decorations.

Wilton Wedding Dream Cakes. This is the ultimate book of wedding cake ideas.

Whimsical Centerpiece, page 18

CHAPTER ONE

The Shower

In olden days, when arranged marriages were common as a way to secure alliances between families—and even countries—dowries were an important tool for fathers to use to lure suitors from the most "attractive" families. Legend has it that the bridal shower originated in Holland when a father, who disapproved of his daughter's upcoming nuptials to a poor miller, refused to give her a dowry. As a result, villagers "showered" her with gifts for her new home.

Now, showers are most typically given by either the maid of honor or another close friend; commonly accepted etiquette states that it is not proper for an immediate family member to give the shower because it may appear as though he or she were asking for gifts.

One popular option is having the shower follow a theme, for instance recipes (where each guest brings a favorite recipe on a card), lingerie, rooms of the house (bathroom, bedroom, kitchen, etc.), and so forth; the host should feel free to use his or her imagination to come up with a special theme that suits the bride's personality and needs. Regardless of what the theme is, though, showers traditionally include games, a light meal and cake, and the making of the bride's rehearsal bouquet from gift bows and ribbons.

Showers for the bride and groom together are becoming more popular; etiquette is changing with the times to include the groom in many of the preparations and celebrations. Now it is common for couples to receive tents, lanterns, and coolers instead of double boilers and toasters!

IN THIS CHAPTER

Whimsical Favors and Photo Album • 16

Hat Place Card • 17

Tiered Ivy Bowl Centerpiece • 17

Whimsical Centerpiece • 18

Bottle Centerpiece • 19

Roses and Hearts Shower Cake • 20

Whimsical Favors and Photo Album

Designed by Carolyn Vosburg Hall
Difficulty level: Easy

Often, at showers and wedding receptions, hosts put cameras on each table for guests to take pictures of each other, but how about giving each guest a packet of cards and a pen to write their thoughts about the special day? These cards can then be used to accompany photos and other memorabilia in this fun photo album.

YOU WILL NEED

Photo Album
Three-ring memory book with purple cover
Pre-cut craft foam hearts in pastel colors
Tacky glue
Scissors
45" of 1" wide sheer satin wire-edge ribbon, purple

Whimsical Favors
4" x 5" pieces of cardstock in pastel colors (use acid-free paper if you are going to use the notes in a photo album)
Gel pens in colors similar to the cardstock
3" x 5" pieces of cardstock, white
28" pieces of 1" wide sheer wire-edge satin ribbon in colors matching the pens
Calligraphy pen or computer
Scissors

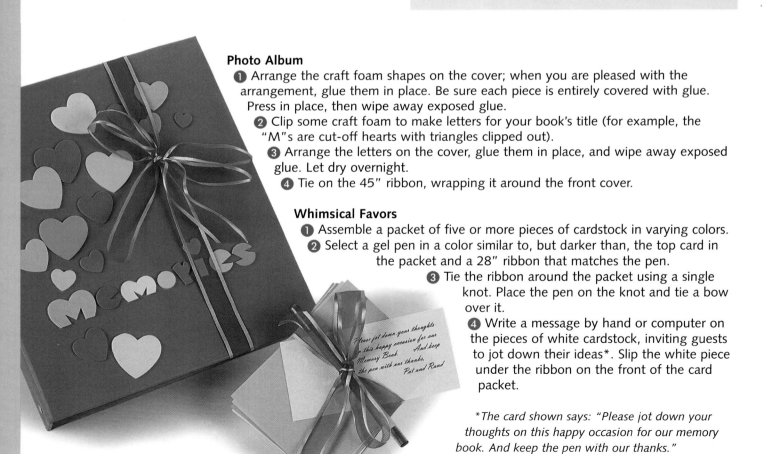

Photo Album

❶ Arrange the craft foam shapes on the cover; when you are pleased with the arrangement, glue them in place. Be sure each piece is entirely covered with glue. Press in place, then wipe away exposed glue.

❷ Clip some craft foam to make letters for your book's title (for example, the "M"s are cut-off hearts with triangles clipped out).

❸ Arrange the letters on the cover, glue them in place, and wipe away exposed glue. Let dry overnight.

❹ Tie on the 45" ribbon, wrapping it around the front cover.

Whimsical Favors

❶ Assemble a packet of five or more pieces of cardstock in varying colors.

❷ Select a gel pen in a color similar to, but darker than, the top card in the packet and a 28" ribbon that matches the pen.

❸ Tie the ribbon around the packet using a single knot. Place the pen on the knot and tie a bow over it.

❹ Write a message by hand or computer on the pieces of white cardstock, inviting guests to jot down their ideas*. Slip the white piece under the ribbon on the front of the card packet.

The card shown says: "Please jot down your thoughts on this happy occasion for our memory book. And keep the pen with our thanks."

Hat Place Card

Designed by Carolyn Vosburg Hall
Difficulty level: Easy

This little decorated hat is a fashionable, easy project your guests will love to take home.

YOU WILL NEED

5 small ribbon roses in pastel colors
Small crocheted hat, 4" across, white
1 yard 5/8" sheer ribbon, pink
7/16" x 8" strip of cardstock, pink
Scissors
Tacky glue
Fine-tip marker, black

❶ To make the hatband, starting 8" from one end, chain the ribbon for 7" (circumference of the hat crown), leaving 8" at the other end. To chain, wrap the ribbon once around your right index finger and twist to make a loop. Pull a second loop of ribbon through the first loop with your forefinger and thumb and pull gently to tighten the loop. Pull the trailing ribbon end through the last loop to hold.
❷ Put a line of tacky glue around the hat crown and place the chained ribbon around the crown to glue it in place.
❸ Tie a bow in the ribbon, leaving 4" tails.
❹ Fold the piece of pink cardstock in the center. Write the guest's name on the paper. Using the edge of the scissors, pull the paper over it to curl both ends. Glue the cardstock's fold to the brim of the hat, under the bow.
❺ Glue three roses to the hatband and one on each ribbon end.

Tiered Ivy Bowl Centerpiece

Designed by Sherry Bartman
Difficulty level: Easy

This simple centerpiece is made in just four easy steps. If you don't care for flowers in the large bowl, replace them with water and a floating flower, candy, accent marbles, or… just use your imagination!

YOU WILL NEED

Large ivy bowl
Small ivy bowl
Assorted flowers, pink
2 wedding bands
1/4" wide ribbon, gold
Tea lite candle
Scissors
Tacky glue

❶ Fill about half of the large bowl with flowers.
❷ Place the small bowl on top of large bowl (it should fit snugly in the opening). Place the tea lite candle inside the small bowl.
❸ Wrap gold ribbon around rim of the large bowl. Glue a small bunch of flowers in the center of the ribbon.
❹ Thread the wedding bands through the ribbon and tie in a bow.

Whimsical Centerpiece

Designed by Carolyn Vosburg Hall
Difficulty level: Easy (but time consuming!)

YOU WILL NEED

Pre-cut craft foam hearts in various sizes and pastel colors
18" x 68" piece of craft foam, yellow
Assorted 12" x 9mm chenille stems in colors to match the craft foam, silver, and white
18" round x 3" high plastic or cardboard container
Floral foam, size to fit in the plastic or cardboard container
5 (or more) 6" x 10" pieces of tulle, white
54" of 1" wide sheer satin-edge ribbon, pink
1-1/2" wide sheer ribbon, purple
2" pins
Scissors
Tacky glue
Clear tape
Floral wire
Bamboo skewer

Not every centerpiece needs to be made of flowers. Here's a playful arrangement of craft foam and chenille stems that has the effect of flowers and is just as easy to make.

1 Push the floral foam into the plastic or cardboard container.

2 From the yellow craft foam, cut one piece 3" x 18", six strips 1/4" x 18", and three strips 3/8" x 18".

3 Make three yellow braids, one with the 3/8" strips and two with the 1/4" strips. Anchor the ends with a 2" pin to keep the foam flat as you braid. When finished, run the braid firmly through your fingers to flatten and stretch it.

4 To make the basket handle, spread one end of the 3/8" braid flat and glue it to one side of the container. Put a piece of clear tape over the end until it dries. Repeat for the other end of the braid. (**Note:** The pieces may need to dry overnight.)

5 Spread glue on the container, wrap the wide craft foam strip around it, and press firmly to make the glue stick. Pin the ends together and tape over the joining to keep it flat. When the glue dries, remove the tape. Put glue on the top edge of the container and wrap a braid around it. Secure the ends with pins and glue. Repeat for the other braid on the bottom of the container. (**Note:** Use scissors to trim off any excess foam so the pieces don't overlap.)

6 To make the fronds, choose approximately four large hearts, four medium hearts, and four small hearts of pre-cut craft foam in the same color. Pierce each in the center with the skewer and thread onto a matching chenille stem 3" from the bottom end. Space the hearts evenly along the stem. Make about nine fronds in assorted pastel colors.

7 Make about ten tendrils from chenille stems of assorted colors (including white and silver) by curling one end into a spiral.

8 Gather each piece of white tulle separately in the center. Tie a wire around the center and twist the ends into a 2" stem.

9 Gather the pink ribbon into a bow, tie it in the center with wire, and twist the stem. Repeat for the purple ribbon.

10 Stick the chenille stems (fronds and tendrils) into the plant foam, half on each side of the basket handle. Stick the tulle wires into the foam, spaced as needed to cover the base. At the front of the arrangement, stick the ribbon wires into the foam.

Bottle Centerpiece

Designed by Sherry Bartman
Difficulty level: Easy

YOU WILL NEED

Large wicker or woven basket
2 bottles of wine, champagne, or sparkling grape juice
Tulle
2" wide ribbon, gold
Caspia
4 small grape clusters
2 large grape bushes
5 flower bushes
4 plant bushes
Scissors
Hot glue gun and glue sticks
Floral foam, size to fit in the center of the basket

Plants are a standard gift for shower guests—but what guest wouldn't love to take home this arrangement complete with two bottles of wine, champagne, or sparkling grape juice?

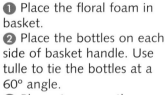 Place the floral foam in basket.
 Place the bottles on each side of basket handle. Use tulle to tie the bottles at a 60° angle.
 Place vines over the handle and around the bottles. Tuck greens evenly around the bottles.
 Add flowers and grapes at random.
 Tie a large bow with the gold ribbon around the handle. Repeat with a large piece of tulle.
 Tack tulle with hot glue around the rim of the basket.

Roses and Hearts
Shower Cake

Designed by Wilton Industries
Difficulty level: Intermediate

Serves 22

With its luscious pink roses and delicate hearts, this one-layer cake will make a statement at any bridal shower.

YOU WILL NEED

12" round x 3" high pan
3, 12, 17, 21, 104, and 352 tips
Colors, Rose and Kelly Green
Buttercream frosting
Royal icing
Flower Nail No. 7
Cake board
Fanci-Foil Wrap, silver
Meringue powder
Waxed paper

❶ In advance, using Royal icing, waxed paper, and the flower nail, make twenty-four tip 104 rosebuds, eleven tip 104 full roses with tip 12 bases, and four tip 104 five-petal roses with tip 12 bases*. Let dry.
❷ Ice the one-layer cake smooth. Pipe the shell top border with tip 17 and the shell bottom border with tip 21.
❸ Randomly pipe tip 3 bead hearts on the top and sides of the cake.
❹ Attach roses and rosebuds with dots of buttercream frosting on the top and left sides of the cake. Add tip 352 buttercream leaves.
❺ Write the message with tip 3.

*For rose instructions, consult one of Wilton Industries' books, listed on page 13.

SHELL

To make shells, hold the bag at an angle so that you can pull the bag toward you. The tip should be slightly above the surface.

Squeezing hard, let the icing fan out generously as it lifts the tip; do not lift the bag. Gradually, relax your pressure as you lower the tip until it touches the surface.

Stop pressure and pull the tip away, without lifting it off the surface, to draw the shell to a point.

To make a shell border, as is needed for this cake, start the end of your next shell so that the fanned end covers the tail of the preceding shell to form an even chain.

HEART

Applying heavy pressure, move the tip slightly and decrease pressure, bringing the end to a point.

Repeat to pipe a second shape, decreasing pressure and joining the tail of the first, forming a "V."

LEAVES

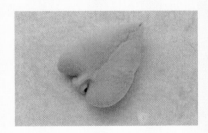

Squeeze hard to build up the base and, at the same time, lift the tip slightly. Relax pressure as you pull the tip toward you, drawing the leaf to a point. Stop squeezing and lift away.

WRITING

Squeeze steadily along the surface in a smooth, continuous motion. Keep your wrist straight, moving your forearm. Use your arm to form each line, letter, or word.

Hand-wrapped Bouquet, page 34

CHAPTER TWO

The Bridal Party

Because the color white has long been thought to symbolize purity, innocence, and affluence, it has been a popular pick for wedding gowns; however, it was not until 1499, when Anne of Brittany chose white for her marriage to Louis XII of France, that it became the color of choice.

As was stated previously, using flowers—and herbs—in a wedding has a long tradition because they represent such things as fertility and purity. The rich scents were thought to discourage evil spirits from pursuing the bride, who has long been seen as a vulnerable target.

Bridal attendants, according to tradition, were also used to ward off evil spirits. The attendants wore clothing similar to the couple in an attempt at confuse the spirits, so they did not know whom to cast a spell on. This camouflage was also used to keep jealous ex-suitors from cursing the couple. And, if they were to see through the disguise, it was the job of the attendants to keep them away.

Long ago, the best man and groomsmen had a very important role: when men had to kidnap or take their brides-to-be from a disapproving family, he would bring along his "best men" to help him fight off other suitors or the woman's male relatives. Around AD 200, the best man also had the job of standing armed, alongside the groom during the ceremony, ready to fend off disapproving relatives. In some churches, tribes would plant clubs, knives, and spears under the altar in case there was an attack!

Today there is little fear of a wedding ceremony being disrupted by evil spirits or angry, armed relatives of the bride, but the role of the attendants has not changed over time: they are there to offer their love and support the bride and groom. While this chapter includes numerous beautiful bouquets for the bride—and boutonnieres for the groom— treat the attendants and other special guests, including parents, grandparents, readers, and musicians, to lovely, easy-to-make arrangements and accessories.

IN THIS CHAPTER

Callas and Satin Arm Sheaf • 24
Callas and Berries Arm Sheaf • 26
Callas and Berries Nosegay • 28
Callas Boutonniere • 30
Callas-trimmed Bag • 30
Callas and Pearl Comb • 31
Lily and Hydrangea Nosegay • 32
Hand-wrapped Bouquet • 34
Periwinkle Scabiosa Cone • 36
Satin Flower Girl Basket • 38
Lily Corsage • 40
Hydrangea Boutonniere • 40
Trimmed Veil • 41
Ribbon and Rose Hair Bow • 42
Rosebud Ring Pillow • 43
Rose Arm Sheaf • 44
Gardenia and Ribbon Bouquet • 46
Orchid Cascade Bouquet • 48
Mixed Cascade Bouquet • 50
Single Orchid Corsage • 52
Double Orchid Corsage • 52
Triple Rose Corsage • 53
Single Rosebud Boutonniere • 53
Pearl and Satin Veil • 54
Pearl and Satin Comb • 55
Trimmed Ring Pillow • 56
Bridal Garters • 57
Raffia-wrapped Bouquet • 58
Cascade Bouquet • 60
Attendant's Basket • 62
Gardenia and Rose Bouquet • 64
Red Rose Bouquet • 66
Red Rose Clutch • 66
Ribbon and Rose Ball • 68
Rosebud Halo • 69
Suede Jewelry Pouch • 70
Bead Strung Jewelry Set • 72

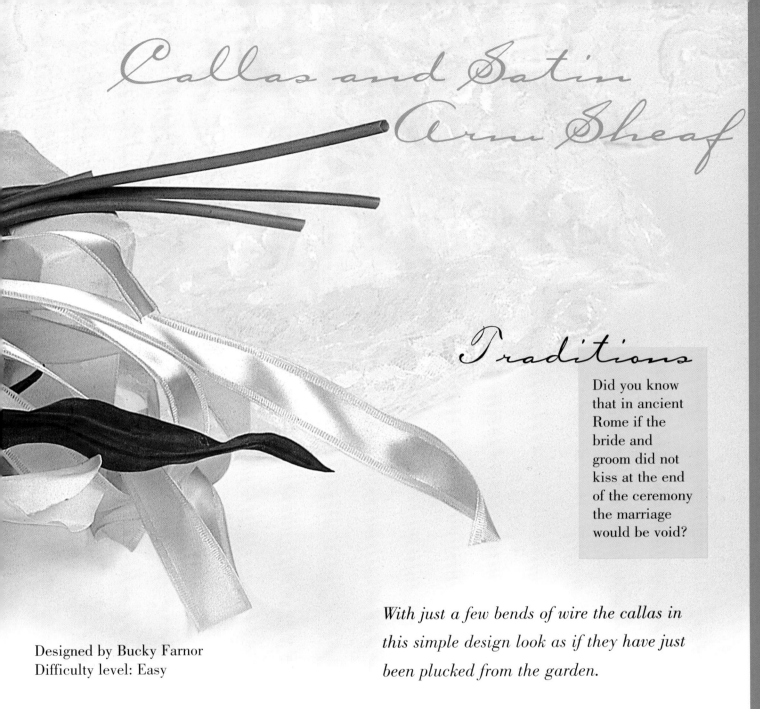

Callas and Satin Arm Sheaf

Traditions

Did you know that in ancient Rome if the bride and groom did not kiss at the end of the ceremony the marriage would be void?

Designed by Bucky Farnor
Difficulty level: Easy

With just a few bends of wire the callas in this simple design look as if they have just been plucked from the garden.

YOU WILL NEED

9 medium callas
Extra leaves
2-1/3 yard 1" wide satin ribbon, white
Floral tape
Scissors
Wire snips

❶ Using floral tape, begin securing the callas, varying the heights. Continue taping the callas together, with the tape in the same place, until you have used all nine.
❷ Fill in any gaps in the design with extra leaves.
❸ Cut 1-1/3 yards from the ribbon. Cut this piece in half and tie the two pieces together to the bouquet, overlapping the tape. Angle off the ribbon ends.
❹ With the remaining ribbon and floral wire, make a multi-loop bow. Secure this bow to the bouquet, over the two knotted ribbons. Angle off the ribbon ends.
❺ To make the bouquet appear more lifelike, manipulate the wires in the callas and leaves by bending them in different directions.
Note: You can either leave the stems so that their lengths vary or you can cut them flush with wire snips.

Callas and Berries Arm Sheaf

Designed by Bucky Farnor
Difficulty level: Easy

At first glance, callas and blueberries may seem like an odd combination, but color-wise, nothing could work better. The navy and white striped ribbon "ties" the entire design together.

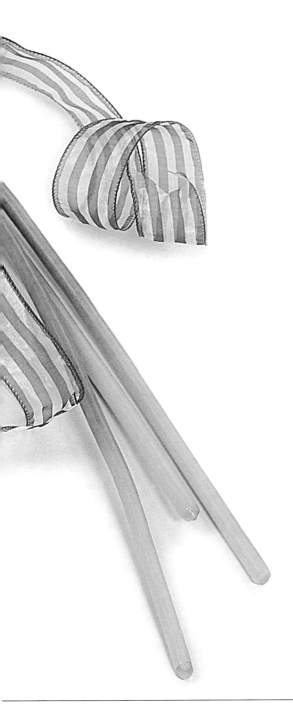

YOU WILL NEED

3 large callas
3 bunches of blueberries, 1 longer than the others
5 feet of 1-1/2" wide wire-edge ribbon, blue and white striped
Floral tape
Floral wire
Hot glue gun and glue sticks
Scissors
Wire snips

❶ Using floral tape, secure the three callas together at varying heights.
❷ Add the bunches of blueberries to the callas with floral tape, with the longest bunch at the top and the two shorter filling in the sides. Wrap floral wire around the stems to add further strength where they are joined.
❸ Cut one foot of ribbon from the entire length. Wrap this piece around the tape that joins the callas and blueberries (over an approximately 3" length); use hot glue, as shown on page 8, to secure the ribbon to the stems.
❹ Using floral wire and the remaining 4-foot piece of ribbon, make a bow and small loop. Cut a "V" in the ribbon ends. Secure the bow to the stems, over the ribbon placed in Step 3.
❺ To make the bouquet appear more lifelike, manipulate the wires in the callas and blueberry bunches by bending them in different directions.

Callas and Berries Nosegay

This delicate bouquet uses the same basic materials as the Callas
and Berries Arm Sheaf on page 26 but on a less grand scale.
Because of its size, it would be perfect for a bridesmaid.

Designed by Bucky Farnor
Difficulty level: Easy

YOU WILL NEED

Approximately 20 small callas
Approximately 12 bunches of small blueberries
2 feet of 1-1/4" wide wire-edge ribbon, blue with white
  polka-dots
Floral tape
Hot glue gun and glue sticks
Wire snips

1 Using floral tape, secure all of the callas and
approximately six bunches of blueberries together.
The single joined stem should be about 5" long
(the bottom 2" will be curled).
2 Fill in the outer areas with approximately six
additional bunches of blueberries, bending them
slightly outward.
3 Using glue as shown on page 8, begin wrapping the
ribbon down the length of the stem, securing the top
2". Glue the end of the ribbon to the stem.
4 Curl the final 2" of the stem.

Callas Boutonniere

This miniature callas arrangement will look stunning on a man's jacket lapel. To add interest to the simple design, bend the wires in the leaves, giving them shape.

Designed by Lisa Vollrath
Difficulty level: Easy

YOU WILL NEED

3 small callas
3 small leaves
Floral tape
Pearl-head pin
Wire snips

❶ Using floral tape, secure the three small callas together at varying heights (the calla in the middle should be tallest, with the one to the left a little higher than the one to the right). Use enough tape so that there is excess at the end to be curled (in Step 3).
❷ Secure the three leaves to the callas, bending the wires, as shown.
❸ Curl the end of the stem.
❹ Add a pearl-head pin for securing the boutonniere to the wearer's jacket.

Callas-trimmed Bag

This darling evening bag is just the right size for such essentials as lipstick, a compact, and breath mints.

Designed by Lisa Vollrath
Difficulty level: Easy

YOU WILL NEED

3 callas
16" of 3/8" wide satin-edge ribbon, purple/blue
Small satin bag embellished with jewels, white
Floral tape
Floral wire
Hot glue gun and glue sticks
Scissors
Wire snips

❶ Using floral tape, secure the three callas together in varying heights.
❷ With 14" of ribbon, tie a bow around the joined stems so that the ribbon ends are pointing toward the callas. Angle off the ribbon ends.
❸ Using floral wire and the remaining 2" of ribbon, add an additional loop of ribbon around the bow made in Step 2.
❹ Hot glue the entire ensemble onto the purse, first at the point where the callas and bow are joined and second behind each of the callas. Glue the ensemble so that the stems are pointing toward the purse's upper left-hand corner.

Callas and Pearl Comb

This callas-embellished comb will look wonderful in any attendant's hair. Because the comb is already covered with pearls, this project can be made quickly and easily.

Designed by Bucky Farnor
Difficulty level: Easy

YOU WILL NEED

Large pearl-covered comb
19 small callas
Hot glue gun and glue sticks
Wire snips

1 Remove the leaves from about half of the callas. When arranging the callas, alternate those with and without leaves.

2 Starting at the upper right corner of the comb, begin gluing and overlapping the callas, so that they point toward the upper right corner.

3 After gluing callas in this fashion for about two-thirds of the comb's length, begin positioning them so that they point toward the lower left corner.

Lily and Hydrangea Nosegay

The addition of faux crystals to a single lily adds just the right amount of sparkle to this monochromatic bouquet.

Designed by Bucky Farnor
Difficulty level: Easy

YOU WILL NEED

1 lily, pink
Approximately 20 bunches of hydrangea with berries, pink
4 yards of 1" wide satin ribbon, pink
2 sprays faux crystals
1 pearl-head pin
Floral tape
Floral wire
Hot glue gun and glue sticks
Scissors
Wire snips

❶ Glue the crystal sprays into the center of the lily.
❷ Using floral tape, join the lily and approximately four bunches of hydrangea. (**Note:** The length of the stem should be approximately 7".)
❸ Continue adding bunches of hydrangea, angling the wires outward so the bouquet forms a circle.
❹ Cut the ribbon in half. Using floral wire, make a large multi-loop bow with one piece of ribbon. Cut a "V" in the ribbon ends. Attach the bow to the base of the stems.
❺ At the base of the stem, covering the place where the bow is attached, begin wrapping the remaining piece of ribbon around the entire length of the stem, securing it with glue as shown on page 8. Wrap the final 2" around the end and secure with a pearl-head pin. Cut a "V" in the ribbon end.
❻ Curl the stem end.

Hand-wrapped Bouquet

Designed by Lisa Vollrath
Difficulty level: Intermediate

YOU WILL NEED

Mix of approximately 30 small and large flowers, including roses and gardenias, all in pastel colors
7-1/2 yards of 6" wide tulle, white
8 yards of 1-1/2" wide wire-edge ribbon, peach
Floral tape
Floral picks
Scissors
Wire snips

Big and glorious, this hand-wrapped bouquet uses a wide array of pastel-colored flowers. To get that "just cut from the garden" look, use a few flowers that have glue "water drops."

❶ Choose one bunch of flowers as the central part of the bouquet. Using floral tape, start adding various flowers around the central bunch. Because this bouquet is hand-wrapped, make sure all of the taping is done in the same place. Leave the stems at about 7" or 8" long.
❷ Fill in the design with bunches of small flowers.
❸ To create the slight cascade of the bouquet, add flowers and stalks with a little length to the round design at the bottom. Bend these flowers and stalks downward.
❹ Fill in any gaps in the design with leaves.
❺ Cut the ends of the stems flush, if desired.
❻ Cut the tulle into four equal-length pieces. Gather each piece in the center and use floral picks to secure each bunch. Using floral tape, add the tulle to the base of the bouquet, equally spaced apart.
❼ Cut the remaining ribbon into three equal pieces. Using floral picks, make three multi-loop bows. Leave long tails on the bow that will be placed at the bottom/central part of the bouquet. Cut a "V" in the ribbon ends. With floral tape, add the three bows at the base of the bouquet.
❽ Glue the remaining piece of ribbon to the base of the bouquet, as shown on page 8. Wrap the ribbon downward to cover the tape. Glue the end of the ribbon to secure.

Periwinkle Scabiosa Cone

Who knew an unusual moss-covered cone could become such an elegant bouquet?
Ribbon loops and flowers hide a Styrofoam ball that helps create the round shape.

Designed by Kim Wakefield
Difficulty level: Advanced

YOU WILL NEED

9" long moss-covered cone
4-1/2" diameter Styrofoam ball
Approximately 30 scabiosas
Approximately 2-1/2 yards of cord, gold
Many yards of sheer satin ribbon, purple
6 pearl-head pins
Metal floral picks
Floral wire
Hot glue gun and glue sticks
Pliers
Scissors
Wire snips

❶ Put a line of glue around the inside rim of the moss-covered cone. Put the Styrofoam ball into the cone. Let the glue dry completely.

❷ With stems about 3" long, begin inserting scabiosas into the Styrofoam ball, leaving some spaces where ribbon loops will fill in. Cover the entire ball with flowers.

❸ For each ribbon "filler," you will need a 5" piece of ribbon and metal floral pick. Make two loops with the ribbon. Put the ribbon ends into the metal floral pick and secure the teeth with pliers, as shown at right. Make as many ribbon loops as needed to fill in all of the gaps in the design. Insert the ribbon loops into the Styrofoam ball.

❹ Cut two 20" long pieces of ribbon and two 20" long pieces of gold cord. Holding one piece of ribbon and one piece of cord together, secure the ends with a metal floral pick. Put the other end in a pick. Insert one end into the Styrofoam ball, where it joins the cone. Wrap the ribbon and cord around the cone and secure on the opposite side with the pick. Repeat with the other piece of ribbon and gold cord, wrapping so that this set overlaps the first, making an "X" on each side of the cone.

❺ Put a pearl-head pin at each intersection ("X") of the two sets of ribbon and cord, two at the sides, and two at the bottom.

❻ To make the handle, cut one 34" long piece of ribbon and one 34" long piece of gold cord. At one side of the cone (between where the "Xs" are), about 8" from one end, secure the ribbon and gold cord together with a pearl-head pin, wrapping the ribbon and cord around and through the pin. Tie a knot in the cord end.

❼ Secure the other end of the ribbon and cord to the opposite side of the cone with the remaining pearl-head pin, leaving approximately 8" of ribbon and cord hanging. Tie a knot in the cord end.

❽ With the remaining gold cord, make two equal length loops (with approximately 10" long cord ends); secure the midpoint with a metal floral pick. Insert the loop picks into the sides of the cone where the handle from Steps 6 and 7 is joined. Tie knots in the cord ends.

Ribbon loop, Step 3.

Satin Flower Girl Basket

Designed by Bucky Farnor
Difficulty level: Easy

YOU WILL NEED

Satin-covered basket, white
Lace, white, in a length that fits around the basket rim
Approximately 35 small roses, pink
Approximately 75 small flowers, purple
4 feet of 1/4" wide eyelet-edge satin ribbon, dark pink
4 feet of 1/4" wide satin ribbon, dark pink
4 feet of 1/4" wide satin ribbon, purple
Floral wire
Hot glue gun and glue sticks
Scissors
Wire snips

Pink and purple flowers and coordinating ribbons add a delightful touch to a white satin basket.

❶ Glue the top of the lace around the entire rim of the basket; you can create "pleats" by overlapping the lace as you glue to give it fullness. In various places, glue the middle of the lace to the basket, allowing the bottom to hang freely.

❷ Covering where the lace is joined to the basket, glue the roses around the basket rim, leaving spaces to fill in with the purple flowers. Save two roses to be used in Step 4 and three or four roses to be used in Step 7.

❸ Fill in the basket rim with purple flowers; continue until the entire rim is covered. Save six flowers to be used in Step 4 and approximately fourteen flowers to be used in Steps 7 and 8.

❹ About 2" away from the handle's center on each side, glue one rose and three purple flowers.

❺ Cut each piece of ribbon in half. Join all four pieces of pink ribbon and the two pieces of purple ribbon; use floral wire to make a multi-loop bow. Angle off the ribbon ends.

❻ Glue the center point of the bow to the bottom of the basket so that the ribbon tails are pointing downward.

❼ Glue the remaining roses and about four purple flowers around the point where the bow is glued to the basket.

❽ Randomly glue the remaining purple flowers to some of the pink ribbons, using two flowers per ribbon (one on the front, one on the back).

Lily Corsage

Designed by Bucky Farnor
Difficulty level: Easy

A large, gorgeous lily is the focal point of this eye-catching corsage. The sprays of faux crystals add sparkle, while the hydrangea and berries complete the look.

YOU WILL NEED

1 lily, pink
3 leaves
3 sprays of faux crystals
9 small hydrangea, pink
3 sprigs of berries, dark pink
8 feet of 1" wide ribbon, dark pink
Floral tape
Floral wire
Scissors
Wire snips

❶ Using floral tape, secure the lily and leaves together. **Note:** The stem should be approximately 4" long.
❷ Join three hydrangea with one sprig of berries; repeat twice for three total bunches. Using floral tape, join the three bunches to the lily, at three equally spaced points.
❸ Add three sprays of faux crystals to the arrangement, in the spaces between the hydrangea bunches.
❹ Cut the ribbon in half. Using floral wire, make two multi-loop bows. Secure one bow to each side of the lily, at the base of the stem. Cut a "V" in the ribbon ends.
❺ Loosely curl the bottom of the stem.

Hydrangea Boutonniere

A boutonniere can simply use the accents from a corsage or bouquet, rather than repeat a focal flower, as in this handsome example.

Designed by Bucky Farnor
Difficulty level: Easy

YOU WILL NEED

6 small hydrangea, pink
2 sprigs of berries, dark pink
4 sprigs of berries, light pink
1 rose leaf
Floral tape
1 pearl-head pin
Wire snips

❶ Using floral tape, secure the six hydrangea together. Make sure to leave enough excess tape at the bottom to be curled in Step 5.
❷ Secure the two sprigs of dark pink berries to the hydrangea.
❸ Add the four sprigs of light pink berries to the arrangement, positioning them above the hydrangea and dark pink berries (giving the boutonniere height).
❹ Secure the rose leaf behind the entire arrangement.
❺ Curl the bottom of the stem.
❻ Add a pearl-head pin for securing the boutonniere to the wearer's jacket.

Ribbon and Hydrangea trimmed Veil

Who says the bride's veil needs to be all white? By adding pink hydrangea and ribbon, this veil has a fresh, spring-like feel.

Designed by Bucky Farnor
Difficulty level: Intermediate

YOU WILL NEED

Headband comb with pearls
17 small hydrangea, pink iridescent
1 small spray of berries, pink
2 yards of 3/4" wide satin ribbon, pink
Two-tiered tulle veil with lace trim
Floral wire
Hot glue gun and glue sticks
Scissors
Wire snips

1 Glue the veil to the inside of the headband.

2 To cover where the veil and headband are joined, glue the spray of berries in the middle.

3 Use the hydrangea to cover the rest of the join until all seventeen are used.

4 Cut approximately 3/4 yard of ribbon. Use this piece of ribbon and floral wire to make a multi-loop bow. Glue the wire to the middle of the headband, over the buds attached in Step 2.

5 Cut the rest of the ribbon into four pieces of varying lengths. Fold each ribbon in half and glue them under the bow.

Traditions

In ancient Greece and Rome, brides would wear red or yellow veils to protect themselves from evil spirits.

Ribbon and Rose Hair Bow

With its delicate pink hydrangea and pretty flowing ribbon, this is the perfect bow to adorn a flower girl's hair.

Designed by Bucky Farnor
Difficulty level: Easy

YOU WILL NEED

1 double-bow satin barrette, white
2 large satin roses, white
7 small hydrangea, pink
3-1/2 yards 1/2" wide satin ribbon, pink
Hot glue gun and glue sticks
Scissors
Wire snips

❶ Using floral wire and ribbon, make one large multi-loop bow. Leave the ribbon ends about 7" long. Angle off the ribbon ends. Cut off any excess wire.
❷ Glue the bow to the top of the barrette, in the middle.
❸ Glue the two roses to the top of the barrette, one on each side of the pink ribbon bow.
❹ Glue the seven hydrangea randomly to the pink bow and barrette.

Rosebud Ring Pillow

Pretty paper roses and rosebuds add simple charm to this pillow.

Designed by Kim Wakefield
Difficulty level: Easy

YOU WILL NEED

Laced-trimmed heart ring bearer's pillow, white
9 paper roses, pink
Approximately 35 paper rosebuds, pink
Extra rose leaves, if needed
1 yard tulle rope, white, with pearls
9 individual pearls
Hot glue gun and glue sticks
Wire snips

❶ Cut 1 foot from the tulle rope. Tie this piece in a bow and glue it to the top of the pillow.
❷ Tie a knot in the middle of the remaining piece of tulle rope; glue to the pillow, just below the bow. This is the piece to which the wedding bands will be tied.
❸ Glue a pearl to the center of each rose.
❹ Starting with one rose at the top, just below the tulle rope, glue the roses and rosebuds around the entire pillow, alternating one rose with bunches of three to four rosebuds. Fill in the pillow with extra leaves, if needed.
❺ When all of the glue is completely dry, secure the wedding bands to the knotted piece of tulle rope; tie in a bow.

In most parts of the world, wedding rings are worn on the third finger of the left hand; the ancient Romans believed this finger had a direct connection to the heart.

Traditions

Rose Arm Sheaf

Designed by Bucky Farnor
Difficulty level: Intermediate

YOU WILL NEED

6 wild roses, white
Approximately 3 berry stems
Fern fronds
Approximately 7 bunches of small hydrangea and berries, pink iridescent
6 yards of 3/4" wide satin ribbon, ivory
Small ivy bush
Floral tape
Floral wire
Scissors
Wire snips

1 Using floral tape, start building the central part of the bouquet with two roses. Add one rose to the right of the two joined roses and three roses above, at varying heights. **Note:** The joined stem should be about 7" long.

2 Start filling in the design with berry stems, above and below the roses.

3 Use the bunches of hydrangea and berries to fill in the design.

4 Add a few fern fronds at the top, bottom, and left-hand side.

5 To create the crescent design, add ivy to both the top and bottom of the design. Bend the ivy to form the crescent shape.

6 Fill in the crescent lines with additional ferns and berries, if needed.

7 When you are finished with the design, wrap floral tape around the entire length of the stem.

8 Cut the ribbon in half. With one piece of ribbon and floral wire, make a large multi-loop bow.

9 Cut the remaining ribbon into three pieces of varying lengths. Fold the three pieces of ribbon in half and secure the midpoints with the wire from the bow. Cut a "V" in the ribbon ends. Put a knot in a few ribbons, a couple of inches from the ends.

10 Secure the bow and ribbons to the bouquet, at the base of the stem.

The combination of wild roses and berries works very well in this crescent-shaped bouquet. To add some color, iridescent pink hydrangea and berries are sprinkled throughout the design.

Traditions

The month of June is named after Juno, the Roman goddess of love and marriage; hence, many have deemed it to be a lucky month during which to marry.

Gardenia and Ribbon Bouquet

Designed by Bucky Farnor
Difficulty level: Intermediate

YOU WILL NEED

6 gardenias (including 2 buds), ivory
6 ranunculus, white
4 yards of 1-1/2" wide satin ribbon, ivory
2 bunches hydrangea and berries, white
Extra leaves
Floral tape
Floral wire
Hot glue gun and glue sticks
Scissors
Wire snips

1. Using floral tape, surround one gardenia with six bunches of hydrangea. **Note:** The final stem length should be about 4" long.
2. Continue building outward from the single gardenia with the six ranunculus, four gardenias, and the two gardenia buds.
3. Fill in any gaps in the design, as well as the outer areas, with extra leaves.
4. Cut 2-1/2 yards from the ribbon. Using floral wire, make a large multi-loop bow with the remaining piece of ribbon. Cut a "V" in the ribbon ends.
5. Secure the 2-1/2-yard piece of ribbon in the bow's wire by folding it in half. Cut a "V" in the ribbon ends.
6. Secure the bow to the stem's base.
7. Tie a loose knot in the long ribbons, about 12" down from the base.
8. Glue the remaining gardenia in the ribbon knot.

Rather than having a cascade of foliage or flowers, this compact design has long, flowing ribbons embellished with a single large gardenia.

Traditions

The beautiful gardenia makes a fitting replacement for roses in wedding arrangements; it represents purity and refinement.

Orchid Cascade Bouquet

Designed by Bucky Farnor
Difficulty level: Intermediate

YOU WILL NEED

5 phalaenopsis orchids
Approximately 12 wild roses, white
5 yards of 3/4" wide satin ribbon, ivory
Small ivy bush
Extra leaves
Floral tape
Floral wire
Scissors
Wire snips

A "traditional" white bouquet does not need to be made solely of roses! Large white orchids mixed with wild roses and ivy steal the show in this cascading design.

1 Begin building the bouquet around one central orchid. Using floral tape, surround the orchid with about five roses. **Note:** The final stem length should be about 6".

2 Add another orchid to the left of the central orchid, one above, and one below. Fill in the design with roses.

3 To create the cascade, add the final orchid and two roses, pointing downward.

4 Use ivy to fill in any final gaps in the design and to add a little height and a lot of length (the ivy should be about 6" longer than the bottom rose) to the bouquet.

5 Fill in any gaps around the central floral design with extra leaves.

6 Cut the ribbon in half. Using floral wire and the two ribbons, make one large multi-loop bow (the ribbon ends should be anywhere from 20" to 25" long). Angle off the ribbon ends.

7 Attach the bow to the base of the stem so that the bow is directly in the back and the ribbons are falling behind the long ivy cascade.

Traditions

Long ago, when females were the property of their fathers, they were literally given away to their husbands, transferring ownership from their fathers. Now, the practice of giving away the bride is symbolic in nature, showing the father approves of and will support the marriage.

Mixed Cascade Bouquet

Designed by Lisa Vollrath
Difficulty level: Intermediate

YOU WILL NEED

1 peony
1 rose, blush
3 roses, buttercream
3 wild roses, white
2 sprays of daisies
1 spray of asters, white
1 spray of hydrangea, green
Bunches of hydrangea, white
2 sprays of wisteria, white
Lilacs, white
Berry sprays, green
Extra leaves
Ivy bush with long trailers
Large bouquet holder
Floral tape
Floral wire
Hot glue gun and glue sticks
Wire snips

Hints of yellow and sprays of green berries add just the right amount of color to this bountiful bouquet. Here, you will be using a bouquet holder on which to create the design.

1 Insert the large blush rose into the center of the bouquet holder. Now begin to fill in the rest of the bouquet holder with the large flowers: one peony, two buttercream roses, and three wild roses. Place these at the top and sides of the holder.

2 Fill in the design with bunches of smaller flowers, including the daisies, asters, and hydrangea, reserving some for the cascade.

3 Use leaves to further fill in the design gaps.

4 Start creating the cascade by inserting daisies, asters, hydrangea, and the remaining buttercream rose into the bottom of the bouquet holder.

5 Insert berry stalks throughout the bouquet, including the top, sides, and cascade.

6 Insert ivy into the bouquet, making the cascade longer than the elements inserted in Step 4. Also fill in the sides of the bouquet with shorter pieces of ivy.

Single Orchid Corsage

Rarely does one flower make a statement, but this stunning orchid needs only minimum embellishment to make it shine.

Designed by Bucky Farnor
Difficulty level: Easy

YOU WILL NEED

1 phalaenopsis orchid
3 leaves
5 feet of 3/8" wide sheer stripe ribbon, ivory
1 looped pearl spray
3 6" tulle circles, white
1 large ivy leaf
Floral tape
Floral wire
Hot glue gun and glue sticks
Scissors
Wire snips

1. With floral tape, sec[...] pearl spray together. A[...] behind the orchid. Use [...] there is excess at the en[...] Step 5).
2. Using ribbon and floral w[...] a large multi-loop bow. Angle [...] the ribbon ends. Secure the bow to the [...]ned orchid, leaves, and pearl spray, at the bottom of the orchid.
3. Gather one piece of tulle in the center. Wrap the center point with floral wire. Repeat for the other two pieces. Secure all three pieces to the back of the arrange-ment.
4. Glue the ivy leaf to the back of the tulle, covering the point where all of the components are joined, as shown.
5. Curl the stem end.

TIP
Use a pearl-head pin to attach any of the arrangements shown on these two pages to the wearer's garment.

Double Orchid Corsage

Two orchids can look just a pretty as one when they are combined with minimal accents. Here, faux crystals add a little sparkle, while ferns give the right amount of color.

Designed by Bucky Farnor
Difficulty level: Easy

YOU WILL NEED

2 phalaenopsis orchids
1 yard of 3/4" wide satin wire-edge ribbon, ivory
3 fern fronds
6 beaded sprays
Floral tape
Floral wire
Scissors
Wire snips

1. For the top part of the corsage, secure one orchid, two ferns, and three beaded sprays together with floral tape.
2. For the bottom part of the corsage, secure the remaining orchid, fern, and beaded sprays together with floral tape.
3. Place the stem of the join from Step 1 over that from Step 2. Secure the two orchids together with floral tape.
4. Using ribbon and floral wire, make a large multi-loop bow. Secure the bow to the corsage, below the bottom orchid. Angle off the ribbon ends.

Triple Rose Corsage

Designed by Lisa Vollrath
Difficulty level: Easy

Here, the combination of three simple white roses, tulle, and ribbon make a lovely corsage.

YOU WILL NEED

1 three-rose spray, white
3 yards of 6" wide tulle
5 feet of 3/8" wide sheer stripe
  ribbon, ivory
Floral tape
Floral wire
Hot glue gun and glue sticks
Scissors
Wire snips

1 With floral tape, secure the three roses together, with one smaller rose at the top and the other two below. Add the three leaves; make sure one is placed between the two lower roses and is pointing directly downward. Use enough floral tape so there is approximately 2" extra that can be curled in Step 5.

2 Cut the ribbon in half. Using the ribbon and floral wire, make two multi-loop bows. Secure the bows to the joined roses, one on either side of the downward pointing leaf. Angle off the ribbon ends.

3 Cut the tulle into three equal pieces. Gather each piece in the middle and secure with a piece of wire. Use the wire to attach the pieces to the corsage, filling in the space between the two bows and adding one piece to each side (and top) of the arrangement.

4 Glue one leaf to the back of the corsage, covering where the roses, leaves, and ribbon are joined, as shown.

5 Curl the stem end.

Single Rosebud Boutonniere

Because boutonnieres do not have to utilize all of the same elements of a bride's bouquet, try adding something unexpected, like berries or twigs, for a fresh look.

Designed by Lisa Vollrath
Difficulty level: Easy

YOU WILL NEED

1 rosebud, white
1 sprig of berries, green
Floral tape
Floral wire
Hot glue gun and glue sticks
Wire snips

1 Cut off the stem of the rose so that it is about 1-1/2" long.

2 Add one cluster of berries to the right side of the rose.

3 Using floral tape, add three leaves to the rose, one to the back and one on each side. Wrap the tape about 1" longer than the rose stem.

4 Curl the stem end.

Pearls are the focus of this grand veil, from the trim around the tulle to the embellished satin flowers.

Designed by Kim Wakefield
Difficulty level: Intermediate

YOU WILL NEED

35 satin roses, ivory, with pearl centers
1 roll tulle rope with pearl trims
2 single veils with ribbon
Pearl-covered headband, white
Hot glue gun and glue sticks
Wire snips

❶ Choose one veil to be embellished with the tulle rope; this will be the top veil. Starting at one side, begin attaching the rope to the veil with glue; carefully glue the rope to the veil at approximate 1-1/2″ intervals.
❷ Glue the remaining veil (ribbon edge facing up) to the inside of the headband, gathering it to fit in an approximate 8″ area.
❸ Glue the embellished veil from Step 1 to the headband, covering the edge of the other veil.
❹ Glue the ivory roses on the headband, covering the entire surface.

Traditions

Veils have typically symbolized virginity, modesty, and respect; it is not to be lifted until after the bride and groom exchange vows.

Pearl and Satin Comb

Pearl sprays lend an elegant feeling to this summery hair comb.

Designed by Kim Wakefield
Difficulty level: Easy

YOU WILL NEED

1 bolt 5/8" wide sheer ribbon with satin edge, ivory
2 bunches satin roses with pearls, white
2 bunches satin rosebuds with pearls, white
3 bunches tulle with pearls, white
Floral wire
Hot glue gun and glue sticks
Scissors
Wire snips

❶ Using the stem wires to secure, join the two bunches of roses together.
❷ Cut the ribbon into five equal lengths. Using floral wire, make five multi-loop bows.
❸ Intersperse the bows throughout the roses joined in Step 1, using the wire to secure. Angle off the ribbon ends.
❹ Again using the stem wires, intersperse the bunches of rosebuds and tulle throughout the roses and bows, filling in the outside areas.
❺ Glue the join of all of the bunches to the comb. Using wire cutters, snip any wire ends flush with the comb's edges.

TIP

It is a good idea for the bride and her attendants to practice their hairstyle with their veil, comb, or other headpiece at least one month before the wedding.

White Ring Pillow

The ring bearer has an important job: walking down the aisle with the bride and groom's wedding rings. This traditional white pillow is the perfect showcase for the rings.

Designed by Lisa Vollrath
Difficulty level: Easy

YOU WILL NEED

Laced-trimmed heart ring bearer's pillow, white
1 pre-made tulle bow, white, in size to cover entire pillow
1 bunch of 3 ranunculus, white
2 pearl sprays, circular
4-1/2 feet of 3/8" wide satin-edge ribbon, ivory
Floral wire
Hot glue gun and glue sticks
Scissors
Wire snips

1. Glue the tulle bow on the pillow, near the top.
2. Glue the two pearl sprays to the ranunculus.
3. Cut 12" from the ribbon. Using floral wire and the remaining ribbon, make a multi-loop bow. Secure the bow to the arrangement made in Step 2.
4. Glue the entire arrangement to the center of the pillow, covering where the tulle bow was glued.
5. Fold the remaining 12" piece of ribbon in half. Glue the ribbon to the pillow, under the flower/pearl arrangement (toward the bottom). Make sure the ribbon is securely glued in place. Angle off the ribbon ends.
6. Secure the wedding bands to the ribbon ends with a knot.

Bridal Garters

Remember the poem "Something old, something new, something borrowed, something blue?"

Even though it is not shown here, many brides choose to add something "blue,"

like a flower, to their garter. Be creative and have fun personalizing yours!

Designed by Sherry Bartman
Difficulty level: Easy

YOU WILL NEED

For Both
Garter
Tulle rope in length to fit around the garter
Rose rope in length to fit around the garter
Sewing needle
Clear nylon thread
Hot glue gun and glue sticks
Scissors

For Small Garter
White ribbon
Pearl ribbon
Pearl for center of flower
1 white flower

For Large Garter
Pearl sprays
Small bunch of white flowers
Wedding bands
Feathers

SMALL GARTER

1 Stitch the tulle rope around the garter, over the elastic; cut any excess. Stitch the rose rope over the tulle rope; cut any excess.
2 Form a bow with the pearl ribbon and stitch it to the front of the garter.
3 Make two bows from white ribbon. Stitch onto the garter, on top of the pearl ribbon bow.
4 Glue the pearl to the flower center.
5 Stitch the flower over the joined ribbons.

LARGE GARTER

1 Follow Step 1 for the Small Garter.
2 Glue the flowers, feathers, and pearl sprays onto the garter.
3 Stitch the wedding bands in the center of the arrangement from Step 2.

Traditions

While the current custom of throwing the bride's garter means the man who catches it will be the next to marry, there are numerous stories about this tradition's origins. One states that the custom began in France, where the bride would toss her garter to guests; whichever guest caught it would be granted happiness and good fortune.

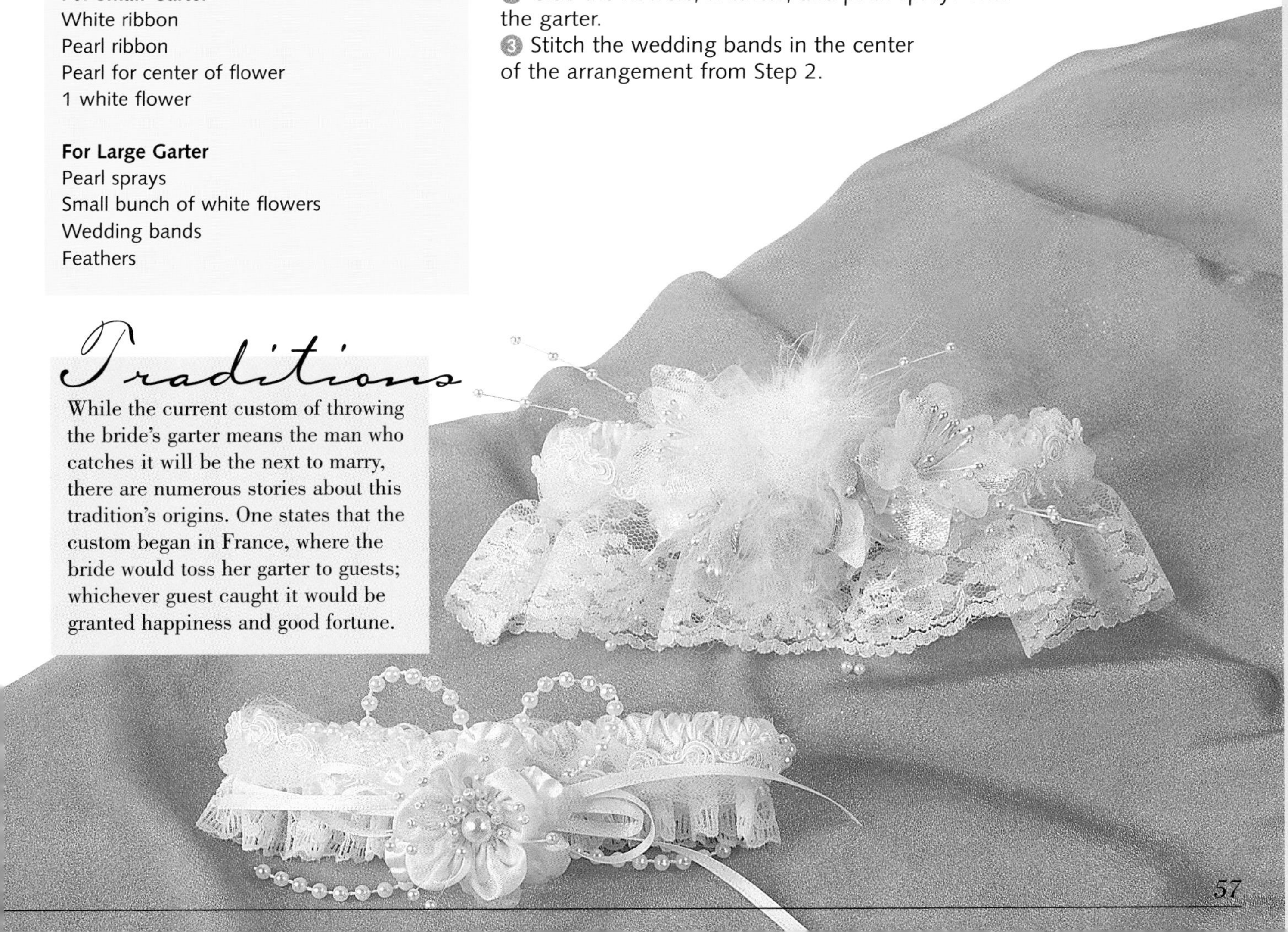

Raffia-wrapped Bouquet

Designed by Lisa Vollrath
Difficulty level: Easy

YOU WILL NEED

3 sunflowers
4 large chrysanthemums, 2 orange and 2 yellow
3 lisianthus, plum
2 peony, plum
6 ranunculus, 3 orange and 3 yellow
Approximately 12 wide leaves
Approximately 3 bunches of berries, dark green and
    yellow
1 bundle raffia, plum
Floral tape
Floral wire
Hot glue gun and glue sticks
Scissors
Wire snips

Sunflowers have long been thought to be a symbol of loyalty. Here, they are combined with an array of fall-inspired colors to create a fun look for a modern bride.

1 Start building the round bouquet with a large flower; using floral tape, begin adding flowers around it to create a round shape until you have used them all. (**Note:** The final stem length should be about 6".) Remember that because this bouquet is hand-wrapped, all of the taping must be done in approximately the same place.

2 After you have added all of the flowers, insert bunches of berries to fill in the design.

3 Fill in the outer edges of the design with the large leaves, leaving a gap in the bottom of the design for the raffia bow.

4 To make the bow, gather a bunch of 24" long raffia; fold in half, overlapping the ends. Secure the middle of the bunch (including the overlapped ends) with floral wire. Pull the raffia strands apart to make them appear fuller. Add the bow to the bottom of the bouquet, in the space left in Step 3.

5 With another 24" long bunch of raffia, cover the place where the floral tape secures the bouquet. Set the raffia on the stem, leaving about 3" pointing downward; wrap the remaining raffia over this section to secure. **Note:** You may want to use glue to help keep the raffia in place.

6 Continue wrapping raffia around the stem. When you are done, tie the ends into a knot and glue in place.

Traditions

In India, in an effort to ward off evil, the groom's brother showers the couple with flower petals at the end of the ceremony.

Cascading Bouquet

Designed by Bucky Farnor
Difficulty level: Intermediate

YOU WILL NEED

10 black-eyed Susans (and buds)
3 zinnias, plum
Approximately 4 rose hip stalks
Assortment of fall leaves, plum, green, and orange
Floral tape
Wire snips

Large plum-colored zinnias and black-eyed Susans are the only flowers used in this cheery autumn bouquet. Rose hips, which are a vibrant burgundy, are the perfect accent.

1 Using floral tape, start building the bouquet with two of the zinnias. Add the remaining zinnia to the left and slightly above the other two. (**Note:** The final stem should be about 5" long.)
2 Fill in the area around the three zinnias with black-eyed Susans.
3 Build the bouquet upward and downward with black-eyed Susans, using buds to round out the design.
4 To add length (the cascade) and height, begin adding the rose hip stalks, extending them beyond the lowest and tallest flowers.
5 Fill in the area around the central bouquet with fall leaves.
6 If there are any gaps, use additional rose hips to fill.

Attendant's Basket

A basket filled with some flowers from the bride's arrangement—along with unexpected fall-harvested apples—is a creative alternative to an attendant's bouquet.

Designed by Bucky Farnor
Difficulty level: Intermediate

YOU WILL NEED

7" round basket
Floral foam, in size to fit inside of basket
2 zinnias, 2 large and 1 small, plum
3 sunflowers
2 stalks of rose hips
2 or 3 stalks of bittersweet
2 apples, one green and one red
Extra leaves
4 yards of 1" wide sheer satin ribbon, plum
Floral wire
2 floral picks
Scissors
Wire snips

1. Put the floral foam into the basket.
2. Put one floral pick in the bottom of each apple. Envision that the basket's handle is the center line (the place where the handles join the basket are the front and back). Put the apples in the basket, one on each side of the center line.
3. With stems about 5" long, add the three zinnias, two at the "front," on one side of the center line, and the other at the "back," on the other side of the center line.
4. Also with stems about 5" long, add the three sunflowers, one at the "front," on the opposite side of the center line from the two zinnias, and the other two at the "back" on at to the left of the center line, opposite the one zinnia.
5. On each side of the basket, insert one stalk of rose hips, bending it outward and downward, and one or two stalks of bittersweet, again bending them outward and downward.
6. Fill in any outer gaps in the design with extra leaves.
7. Cut the ribbon in half. With floral wire and the two pieces of ribbon, make a multi-loop bow; leave the ribbon ends anywhere from 12" to 18" long. Angle off the ribbon ends. Insert the bow into the foam at the front of the design, between the front sunflower and rose hips.

Gardenia and Rose Bouquet

Designed by Bucky Farnor
Difficulty level: Intermediate

YOU WILL NEED

4 gardenias, white
2 gardenia buds, white
Approximately 7 bunches of small satin roses, red
Approximately 5 stalks of berries, red
2 feet of 1" wide sheer satin ribbon, red
5 pearl-head pins
Ivy
Floral tape
Hot glue gun and glue sticks
Scissors
Wire snips

The red berries in this bouquet sparkle in the light—imagine how they would shine in an evening candle-light ceremony!

❶ Begin building the bouquet from the top, with one small gardenia; join the three other gardenias to it, varying their heights (two large on the sides and the remaining small at the bottom). **Note:** The joined stem should be approximately 6" long.

❷ Next add approximately four clusters of small red roses between the gardenias.

❸ Start building the cascade by adding the two gardenia buds. Continue to build downward with approximately three rose clusters.

❹ Begin adding berries, first at the top part of the bouquet and then downward toward the cascade. Use the berries to fill in the gaps between the gardenias and roses.

❺ Add ivy, giving height to the top and length to the cascade. Fill in the side of the bouquet sparingly with shorter pieces.

❻ Begin wrapping ribbon around the stems, starting at the base. Glue the ribbon end as shown on page 8; you can add extra support by inserting a couple of pearl-head pins into the ribbon-wrapped stem. Wrap ribbon down the entire 6" stem length. When you get to the end of the stems, leave a 2" tail, and secure with a pearl-head pin (this goes directly into the stems' end). Angle off the ribbon end.

Red Rose Bouquet

This bouquet includes three rosebuds at the bottom, which add a special finishing touch.

Designed by Bucky Farnor
Difficulty level: Easy

YOU WILL NEED

10 rosebuds, red
4 large roses, red
Approximately 9 sets of rose leaves
1 yard 1" wide sheer satin ribbon, red
1 pearl-head pin
Floral tape
Hot glue gun and glue sticks
Scissors

❶ With floral tape, secure the four large roses around one rosebud.
❷ Add three two-rosebud groups around the arrangement, in a triangle form.
❸ Surround the roses with approximately nine sets of leaves, filling in any gaps in the arrangement.
❹ With floral tape, secure the three remaining rosebuds together. Join these three rosebuds to the bouquet arrangement, with their stems pointing toward the bouquet. There should be approximately 7" between the bouquet and rosebuds.
❺ Begin wrapping the ribbon around the stems, starting at the base of the bouquet arrangement. Glue the ribbon end as shown on page 8.
❻ Wrap ribbon down the entire stem length, about 1" above the three end rosebuds. Wrap the ribbon back up the stem for about 2", leave a 1" tail, and secure with a pearl-head pin. Cut a "V" in the ribbon end.

Red Rose Clutch

This simple attendant's bouquet is the perfect complement to the Red Rose Bouquet; it uses the same four large roses but no rosebuds. The curled ribbon-wrapped stem adds an interesting line to the arrangement.

Designed by Bucky Farnor
Difficulty level: Easy

YOU WILL NEED

4 large roses, red
Approximately 4 sets of rose leaves
2 yards of 1" wide sheer satin ribbon, red
Floral tape
1 pearl-head pin
Hot glue gun and glue sticks
Scissors

1 Using floral tape, secure the four roses together. Leave the stems on two of the roses about 18" long.

2 Add the leaf clusters, filling the spaces around the roses.

3 Begin wrapping ribbon around the stems, starting at the base of the roses and leaves. Glue the ribbon end as shown on page 8.

4 Wrap ribbon down the entire 18" stem length. When you get to the end of the stems, wrap back up the stem for about 1-1/2", leave a 1" tail, and secure with a pearl-head pin. Cut a "V" in the ribbon end.

5 Curl the stem end.

Ribbon and Rose Ball

Bouquets don't need to be made entirely of flowers! This elegant arrangement is made up of ribbon bows, with small accent flowers and pearls that add color and interest.

Designed by Lisa Vollrath
Difficulty level: Intermediate

YOU WILL NEED

6" Styrofoam ball
Many yards of 1" wide sheer satin ribbon, red; reserve a 1-foot piece for Step 5
2 yards of pearls
Approximately 30 flowers with pearl sprays, white
Approximately 30 paper rosebuds, red
Floral wire
1 metal floral pick
Hot glue gun and glue sticks
Scissors
Wire snips

❶ Cut dozens of 8" pieces of ribbon. Using floral wire, make enough four-loop bows to cover the entire Styrofoam ball. (You will need about sixty bows.)

❷ Glue a rosebud into the center of approximately half of the bows.

❸ For the remaining bows, glue a white flower into the center.

❹ Insert the bow wires into the ball, covering the entire surface.

❺ Cut a 1-foot piece from the pearl strand. Use this piece and a 1-foot piece of ribbon; form a loop (handle) for the top of the ball. Secure the ends in a metal floral pick. Push the pick into the top of the ball.

❻ For the bottom of the ball, make a bow with the remaining pearl strand. Secure the center with a piece of floral wire. Push the wire into the bottom of the ball; glue the pearl bow in place, if necessary.

Rosebud Halo

Nothing exemplifies childhood innocence more than this angelic-looking halo.
Adjust the length of the ribbon streams to suit the length of the flower girl's hair.

Designed by Bucky Farnor
Difficulty level: Easy

YOU WILL NEED

Approximately 16 roses, red*
Approximately 17 flowers,
   white*
2 yards of 1" wide sheer satin
   ribbon, red
Floral tape
Floral wire
Scissors
Wire snips

*You will need more or less depending on
the size of the halo

❶ Measure the crown of the wearer's head. Using this measurement, you will make three equal length floral pieces to be joined in a circle.

❷ To make each section, using floral tape, join roses and white flowers, alternating one rose with one white flower. Repeat this procedure for all three sections.

❸ Join two sections from Step 2 with floral wire for added stability. Add the final section, bending the sections to form a circle. Cover the wire joins with additional floral tape.

❹ Cut the ribbon in half. Together, tie the two pieces of ribbon around the halo; form a knot. Cut a "V" in the ribbon ends.

Suede Jewelry Pouch

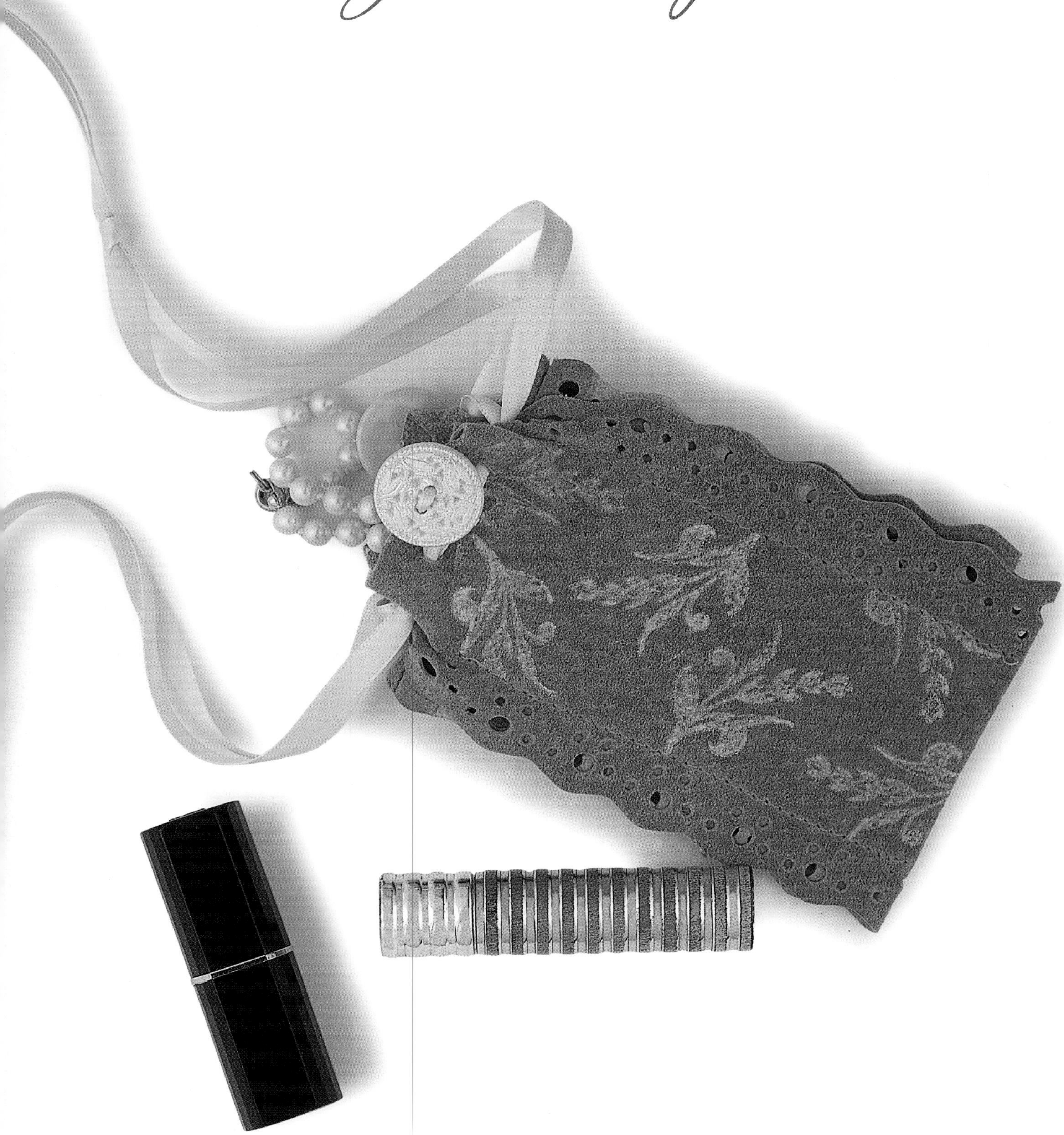

Designed by Kari Lee for The Leather Factory
Difficulty level: Intermediate

YOU WILL NEED

2 pieces of Pewter Velvet Suede Trims from The Leather Factory
Tanners Bond Leathercraft Cement from The Leather Factory
Poly Mallet from The Leather Factory
6" x 6" x 1/2" Punch and Cutting Board from The Leather Factory
Mini Punch Set from The Leather Factory
Sprig Engraving stamp from Rubber Stampede
45mm rotary cutter and wavy blade
2 yards of 3/8" wide ribbon, ivory
2 buttons, ivory
Fabric or acrylic paint, white
Sponge applicator
Ruler or straight edge
3" x 5" self-stick notes
Tape (1" piece)
Paper clips
Scissors
Polyester thread (to match suede)
Sewing machine with leather needle or glovers needle for hand stitching

This pretty suede jewelry pouch is perfect for the bride to give as a gift to her bridesmaids or to hold her jewelry that is to be worn on that special day. The pouch provides ample room with two separate compartments for earrings, a necklace, or bracelet—or even such small items as lipstick. The surface of the pewter-colored suede has a decorative stamped pattern, complemented with a perforated and wave-cut edge.

Step 2   Step 2   Step 6

❶ Along the center of the two suede trim pieces, create a 2" margin to be decoratively stamped, using self-stick notes to mask the edges.

❷ Thoroughly apply white fabric or acrylic paint on the rubber stamp image with a sponge applicator. Randomly stamp the image along the center of the suede trim pieces, reapplying paint onto the rubber stamp after each impression, as shown. Let dry.

❸ Using the rotary cutter with the wave blade and a straight edge as a guide, cut along the length of both suede trim pieces.

❹ Position the stamped sides of the suede trim pieces together. Machine or hand stitch (with a glovers needle) one end together, creating one continuous length. Adhere the seam open with Leathercraft Cement.

❺ Place the suede length face up on the punch board surface. To create the perforated design along the wave cut edges, two sizes of tubes will be used on the punch handle. First, attach the #3 tube onto the handle. With a mallet, begin to punch the singular large decorative holes along the wave edge, starting

and ending with the second full wave, about 3/4" from the end. Then punch four holes equally spaced apart and approximately 3/8" from the end for the ribbon closure.

❻ To complete the perforated decoration, attach the #0 tube onto the handle and punch four holes around each large hole, as shown.

❼ Fold the suede length in half at the seam with the suede sides together. Fold the remaining length on both sides with the suede side showing and over the top seam edge about 3/4" (or to the second wave).

❽ Match the waves as much as possible along the edges and secure with paper clips. Using the stamped pattern as a guide, machine or hand stitch along the four edges, creating the two pockets for the pouch.

❾ Cut two 36" lengths of ribbon. Wrap a piece of tape around one end of each ribbon length and cut to a point; take off the tape. Thread each ribbon through the holes and a button along the top edge of bag from opposite sides of pouch. Tie a knot with the loose ends of each ribbon to complete the closure.

Finished Measurements
Necklace: 3 strands, 18", 16-1/2",
and 15-1/2"
Bracelet: 8"
Earrings: 1-3/4"

Use this diagram as the bead
pattern (for stringing order).

Bead String Jewelry Set

This classy jewelry set is the perfect (inexpensive) gift for attendants—for about $30, you can make three complete sets!

Designed by Jane Davis
Difficulty level: Easy

YOU WILL NEED

Natural amethyst semi-precious stone heart
Opaque E beads, lavender
Size 10 rochaille beads, purple
Small faceted beads, off-white
Large oval beads, purple
Large freshwater pearls, white
Small freshwater pearls, blue/gray
Clasp, toggle clasp, and spacers
Small sterling silver ear wire
White beading thread
Beading needle
Glue
Scissors

Necklace

❶ Cut a 4-foot length of thread. Pass the thread through one of the holes on the large clasp and tie a square knot so that the clasp is knotted in the middle of the thread. Thread both tails with the needle so that you are working with a doubled thread.

❷ String the bead pattern shown for one strand of the necklace and remove the needle.

❸ Pass one thread through the corresponding hole on the other part of the clasp and tie both thread ends with a square knot, tightening the beads on the strand. Rethread the tails and pass them back through the strand for about 2". Cut close to the beadwork. Dab a small amount of glue on the knots.

❹ Repeat the process for the other two strands.

Bracelet

❶ Cut a 2-foot length of thread. Pass the thread through the toggle end of the toggle clasp and tie a square knot so that the toggle is knotted in the middle of the thread. Thread both tails with the needle so that you are working with a doubled thread.

❷ Repeat Steps 2 and 3 for the necklace, following the bead pattern for the bracelet.

Earrings

❶ Cut a 12" length of thread. Tie the thread to the loop of the ear wire with a square knot, leaving a 4" tail. Thread the needle with the long end of thread and string the bead pattern for the earring.

❷ Pass the needle and thread back through all of the beads, except the last one strung.

❸ Tie the tail thread and the working thread into a square knot and then pass them back through the beads. Cut close to the beads. Dab a small amount of glue on the knot.

❹ Repeat Steps 1 through 3 for the second earring.

TIP
Square knots are often used in beading. To make a square knot, cross the thread in your right hand over the thread in your left hand and around and through to tie a knot. Then, cross the thread that's now in your left hand over the thread in your right hand and around and through to tie a knot again. This makes a secure knot that won't slip out as easily as others.

Fall Harvest Altar Arrangement, page 84

CHAPTER THREE

The Ceremony

CEREMONIES HAVE BECOME more elaborate as times have passed. It wasn't until the medieval period that the priest was even necessary! Before that it was sufficient for the couple to agree to spend the rest of their lives together, but sometimes they would invite a priest to bless the marriage.

The walk down the aisle was once littered with flower petals that children used to keep evil spirits from rising from below and cursing the bride. Today the presence of children adds a tone of innocence to the ceremony. In many weddings, a young boy is trusted with the important task of bringing the rings to the altar.

Music has been constant since Princess Victoria married Price Frederick William of Prussia in 1858. At the time, it was simply Victoria's choice. Today, Wagner's "Bridal Chorus" has become a Western tradition for the bride's walk down the aisle.

These days, the father "gives away the bride" not as an exchange of property, but as a token of his blessing. And the kiss, originally signifying the legal bond that closes the deal, has become a romantic finale to the couple's vows.

After the ceremony is over and the newlyweds get into their decorated car, guests blow their horns to salute the couple's new life together. This joyous tradition has replaced an old custom where the guests made loud noises during the ceremony, again to deter evil spirits.

One thing that hasn't changed is the tradition of placing a six pence in the bride's shoe as a wish for wealth. A penny suffices for weddings in the United States, but now the bride who's not taking any chances can purchase a silver six pence on the Internet!

IN THIS CHAPTER

Unity Candle Holder • 76
Heart Pew Bow • 77
Unity Candle Set • 78
Garden Altar Arrangement • 80
Ranunculus Pew Bow • 82
Braided Pew Bow • 83
Fall Harvest Altar Arrangement • 84
Layered Invitation • 86
Perfect Programs • 87

Unity Candle Holder

Designed by Bucky Farnor
Difficulty level: Intermediate

Traditionally, the unity candle is much larger in diameter than the two candles used to light it; however, in this case, it is simply a longer taper.

YOU WILL NEED

6-1/4" x 4" x 2" block of Styrofoam
1-1/3 yard of 2-1/4" wide wire-edge satin ribbon, ivory
4 yards of 1/2" satin ribbon, pink
3 taper candles, white, 1 being taller than the others
1 large rose, dark pink
2 rosebuds, dark pink
2 small roses, light pink
Approximately 5 sprigs of berries, white and pink
Approximately 10 sprigs of eucalyptus, plum
Many sprays of geranium leaves
Sharp pointed object
Metal floral picks
Hot glue gun and glue sticks
Scissors
Wire snips

❶ Cut two pieces of ivory ribbon, each about 8-1/2" long. Lining up the ribbon edge with the bottom of the Styrofoam block, glue one piece of ribbon to the block. Use the second piece of ribbon to cover the exposed top, overlapping the first.
❷ With the remaining piece of ivory ribbon, glue one end to the back of the Styrofoam block. Wrap the ribbon around the block and to the back, securing the other end with glue

(cut any excess more than 2" prior to gluing). This piece will cover the ribbon ends secured in Step 1.
❸ For placement, push the tall candle into the top of the block, in the center and about 1" from the back edge; make the indent about 3/4" deep. Push the two small candles into the top of the block, about 1-1/2" to the left and right of the tall candle. Pull out the candles.
Note: From Step 4 through the end, you will need to attach a metal floral pick to each flower, leaf, etc. If you have difficulties inserting the picks into the Styrofoam block covered with ribbon, use the sharp pointed object to pierce the ribbon.
❹ Insert the large rose in the top of the block, directly in the center.
❺ Put one small light pink rose on each side of the large rose.
❻ Insert one rosebud at each side of the block.
❼ Fill in the front and sides of the arrangement with leaves, leaving some space for berries at the front and sides and eucalyptus at the sides.
❽ In the spaces left in Step 7, insert the berries around the roses and at the sides of the arrangement.
❾ Now fill in the back of the foam with leaves, making sure not to cover the holes made by the candles in Step 3.
❿ To complete the design, put eucalyptus on each side of the block.
⓫ Cut two pieces of ribbon, each 24" long. Using the remaining ribbon and floral wire, make a multi-loop bow. Angle off the ribbon ends.
⓬ Fold the two pieces of remaining ribbon in half. Secure these ribbons in the multi-loop bow's wire.
⓭ Insert the bow into the top of the block, directly in back of the large central rose.
⓮ Insert the candles into the top of the block, in the holes made in Step 3.

Heart Pew Bow

Designed by Bucky Farnor
Difficulty level: Intermediate

Yards of pink ribbon and iridescent hydrangea make this simple pew bow a pretty addition to any ceremony.

YOU WILL NEED

5" tall Styrofoam heart
7 yards of 1/2" wide satin ribbon, pink
Approximately 35 small hydrangea, iridescent pink
7 yards of tulle, white
Floral wire
Hot glue gun and glue sticks
Scissors
Wire snips

1 Glue one end of the pink ribbon to the Styrofoam heart. Tightly wrap the ribbon around the heart; when finished, cut the ribbon and glue the end to the heart.

2 Glue the iridescent hydrangea all around the ribbon-wrapped heart, reserving six for later use.

3 Cut a piece of ribbon approximately 3 yards long. Using this ribbon and floral wire, make a multi-loop bow, leaving approximate 6" ends. Leave excess wire to secure the bow to the pew.

4 Cut the remaining ribbon into three pieces of varying lengths. Fold each piece in half and attach to the multi-loop bow with the floral wire. Angle off the ribbon ends.

5 Knot the ends of half of the ribbons. Glue a hydrangea just above each knot.

6 Glue the bow to the bottom tip of the ribbon-covered heart.

7 Using the tulle, create eight bows with 5-1/2" loops. Then make one large bow.

8 Wrap the ends of the wire from the multi-loop bow around the center of the tulle bows.

9 Allow one end of the tulle to hang down from the heart about 3 feet. Cut a "V" in the tulle ends. Tuck the other end into the wire.

10 Carefully spread the tulle bows so that the smaller bows poof up behind the heart, and the longer bows and tulle "tails" hang down from the heart.

11 Secure the excess wire from Step 3 to the pew.

Unity Candle Set

The theme of "two becoming one" is apparent throughout this design: the main arrangement sits atop a double wedding ring candle holder, while each side taper is supported by a single ring.

Traditions

Unity candles symbolize the coming together, or unity, of the bride's and groom's families; when the two tapers are used to light the larger unity candle, the families become one.

Designed by Lisa Vollrath
Difficulty level: Advanced

YOU WILL NEED

The two side arrangements:
2 brass single-ring taper holders
2 9" tapers, white
6 ranunculus
8 leaves
2 yards of 3/8" wide sheer stripe ribbon, ivory
Floral tape
Floral wire
Scissors
Wire snips

The main arrangement:
Brass double-ring candle holder
Brass pillar holder
4" x 3" x 3" foam block
Floral foam sheet moss
S pins
2 large roses, white
1 rose, peach
2 rosebuds, peach
2 ranunculus sprays
Green berries
Ivy bush
Small daisies
8 15" x 3-1/2" pieces of tulle, white
4 circular pearl sprays
2 32" strands of pearls
9" tall pillar candle, ivory
4 yards of 3/8" wide sheer stripe ribbon, ivory
32" of 1-1/2" wide rose-embossed satin ribbon, ivory
Floral wire
Hot glue gun and glue sticks
Scissors
Wire snips
Optional: Metal floral picks

Two Side Arrangements

Note: Follow the instructions to embellish one of the tapers; repeat to embellish the other.

1 Using floral tape, secure three ranunculus together. You will need an approximate 4" stem.

2 Add four leaves of varying lengths to the ranunculus.

3 Cut the ribbon in half. Use one piece and floral wire to make a multi-loop bow. Using floral tape, secure the bow to the ranunculus.

4 Wrap the joined stem of all of the components around the base of the taper holder.

5 Insert one taper into the holder.

Main Arrangement

1 Cover all four sides of the foam block with moss. Glue the brass pillar holder to the top of the foam, directly in the center.

2 Designate one side of the foam to be the front and one to be the back. Starting at the back of the foam, directly in the middle, insert the large white rose. On the front, insert the large peach rose, just to the right of center, and two ranunculus to

the left. **Note:** If you have difficulties inserting any of the elements into the moss-covered foam, use metal floral picks to aid you.

3 With the foam's front facing you, insert the smaller white rose into the left side. Insert one peach rosebud into the right side.

4 With the front still facing you, insert one peach rosebud into the left side, below the white rose.

5 Insert a few sprays of daisies into the sides.

6 Now turn the design around so that the back is facing you. Insert the remaining peach rose into the foam, to the right of and above the white rose.

7 Insert the two remaining ranunculus into the foam, to the left of and below the rose.

8 With the back still facing you, insert the remaining daisy sprays into the sides of the foam.

9 Gather one piece of tulle in the center and secure with floral wire. Repeat for the remaining pieces. Insert the tulle into the foam, around the pillar holder on top, two pieces beside the white rose on the back, and the remaining pieces in the front, near the peach rose and ranunculus.

10 Insert green berries into the sides of the design, one stalk on each side, and fill in the gaps in both the front and back of the design with ivy. Use the ivy to add length to the sides of the design.

11 With the front of the foam facing you, add three pearl sprays, two near the peach rose and one on the left side, near the white rose.

12 Turn the foam around to the back. Insert one pearl spray on each side of the white rose.

13 Cut the 3/8" ribbon into four equal-length pieces; angle the ribbon ends. Using floral wire and one piece of ribbon, make a multi-loop bow with approximate 9" tails. Make another multi-loop bow with another piece of ribbon. Insert one bow into each side of the foam.

14 Fold one of the remaining pieces of ribbon in half, along with one of the pearl strands; secure the two together with floral wire. Repeat for the final piece of ribbon and pearl strand. Insert one ribbon and pearl piece into each side of the design, below the bow. To help secure the ribbon and pearl further, you can use small pieces of wire to attach them to the ivy at long intervals.

15 Secure the foam to the candle holder with glue.

16 Cut the rose-embossed ribbon into four equal-length pieces. Glue the end of one piece on the candle, so that the top edge of ribbon is about 1-1/2" below the top of the candle. Wrap the ribbon around the candle. Fold over the end of the ribbon and glue in place.

17 With another piece of ribbon and floral wire, make a bow; the ends should be short enough to "hide" under the bow. Cut off any excess. Glue a daisy to the bow, covering the floral wire.

18 Repeat Steps 16 and 17 with the remaining pieces of ribbon and daisy, with the new wrapped ribbon being about 1-1/2" below the piece from Step 16.

19 Place the candle on the brass pillar holder.

20 Place one side arrangement on each side—or in front—of the main arrangement.

Garden Altar Arrangement

Designed by Bucky Farnor
Difficulty level: Advanced

YOU WILL NEED

8 open roses, white
2 bunches double-ruffle, white
3 peonies with buds, white
4 delphiniums, white
1 French rosebud, white
3 French roses, white
5 bunches forget-me-nots, white
5 delphinium sprays, white
4 bunches plum blossoms, white, with leaves
3 bunches mini-tiger lilies, white
3 gardenia sprays, white
3 peonies, white
Floral foam, in size to fit in vase
1-foot tall vase, white
Wire snips

Note: It is easier to freeform this arrangement than give specific instructions; follow the basic look of the arrangement pictured.

1. Insert the floral foam into the vase.
2. Start in the center of the design by inserting the tallest flowers into the foam.
3. Start building outward with shorter flowers.
4. Continue decreasing the height of the design by adding shorter roses and lilies.
5. Add some longer elements to the bottom of the design and bend them outward and downward so that they cover the upper portion of the vase.
6. Fill in any gaps in the design with foliage.

Tall and lush, this arrangement is full of the summer garden's bounty, from roses and peonies to delphinium sprays and tiger lilies.

Traditions

While June is the most popular month of the year during which to marry, all of the summer months are traditionally thought to be good times because the sun is a symbol of fertility.

Designed by Bucky Farnor
Difficulty level: Intermediate

Creamy ranunculus and thick satin ribbon are combined for an elegant pew bow that resembles a bouquet.

YOU WILL NEED

10 ranunculus
5 yards tulle, ivory
7 yards 2-1/2" wide wire-edge ribbon, ivory
White floral tape
Floral wire
Hot glue gun and glue sticks
Scissors
Wire snips

1 Cut the tulle in half. Overlap the two pieces of tulle and, using floral wire, make a multi-loop bow with long tails. Cut a "V" in the tulle ends.

2 Cut the ribbon in half. Use one piece and floral wire to make a large multi-loop bow.

3 Cut the remaining piece of ribbon into two pieces, with one being longer than the other. Fold the two pieces in half and secure them to the multi-loop bow with floral wire. Cut a "V" in the ribbon ends.

4 Using the floral wire from the tulle bow and multi-loop ribbon bow, join them together securely, with the tulle behind the ribbon.

5 Cut the stems of the ranunculus to about 2" and glue them randomly among the ribbon loops. You can create a cascade look by grouping approximately five flowers together at the bottom, pointing downward.

BASIC PEW BOW

Making a pew bow is easy!
1 *Leaving a ribbon tail, gather one loop of ribbon.*

2 *Twist the ribbon and form another loop. Continue twisting the ribbon and forming loops until you have a tail that is the same length as the other.*

3 *Use a piece of floral wire to secure the loops; twist the wire to tighten.*

Braided Pew Bow

Designed by Bucky Farnor
Difficulty level: Intermediate

Breezy pre-made sheer white rosettes and carefully braided ribbon will make a truly elegant statement when placed on any pew.

YOU WILL NEED

5 pre-made sheer rosettes, white
12 yards of 2-1/2" wide wire-edge satin ribbon, white
Floral wire
Scissors
Hot glue gun and glue sticks
Wire snips

1. Cut a piece of ribbon that is approximately 5 yards long. With this piece and floral wire, make a large multi-loop bow.
2. Randomly glue the sheer rosettes to the bow.
3. Cut three pieces of ribbon in the following lengths: two 22" and one 30". Use floral wire to secure one end of each piece to the bottom of the multi-loop bow. Cut a "V" in the ribbon ends.
4. Cut the remaining ribbon into nine pieces, in three groups of three ribbons of equal length (do not cut all pieces to the same length).
5. Braid each group of three ribbons. When finished, fold each braid in half, so that the loop points downward. Gather the three braids together and secure the ends with floral wire.
6. Using the floral wire from the multi-loop bow and braids, join them together, twisting the wire to secure. Leave enough excess wire to attach the bow to the pew.

Fall Harvest Altar Arrangement

Designed by Bucky Farnor
Difficulty level: Advanced

YOU WILL NEED

12" tall bucket, green
Floral foam, in size to fit in bucket
Tall grasses
6 stalks of bittersweet
4 stalks of rose hips
Sunflowers
Zinnias, yellow and plum
Marigolds, yellow and orange
Apples, green and red
Floral picks
Wire snips

Standing nearly 5 feet tall, this is the ultimate altar arrangement. After the ceremony, this would make a grand piece to use in the foyer of your home.

Note: It is easier to freeform this arrangement than give specific instructions; follow the basic look of the arrangement pictured.

1 Put the floral foam into the bucket.
2 Start in the center of the design by inserting tall grasses into the foam.
3 Next, start building outward with shorter stalks of bittersweet and rose hips.
4 Continue decreasing the height of the design by adding shorter zinnias, sunflowers, and marigolds. Add a lot of fullness around the base of the design with numerous flowers.
5 Add some long bittersweet and rose hip stalks to the left and right sides of the design and bend them downward so that they cover the container; do not fill the area in the center with long elements.
6 Insert floral picks into the bottom of the apples. Fill in any gaps in the design with the apples.

Traditions

Zinnias, which come in many colors including magenta and yellow, are an ideal flower to use in wedding arrangements; they symbolize lasting affection and daily remembrance.

Layered Invitation

Vellum is a beautiful, dainty paper. When combined with ordinary cardstock and sheer ribbon, it creates a simple, yet effective, invitation. Making the envelope is a breeze with some simple folds and decorative-edge scissors. You can easily make enclosure cards with additional cardstock.

Designed by Blanche Lind
Difficulty level: Intermediate

YOU WILL NEED

5-5/8" x 5-3/4" piece of cardstock, lilac
5-1/2" x 5-1/2" piece of vellum
5-1/2" x 5-1/2" pieces of typing paper
6" of 1" wide sheer ribbon, lilac
8-1/2" x 14" cardstock, white
Scissors
Decorative-edge scissors
Hole punch
Glue stick
Computer and printer

❶ Type the text on a computer; carefully check spelling and grammar. Try different fonts to see which is most appealing (Park Avenue is shown). Print samples on pieces of 5-1/2" x 5-1/2" typing paper to double-check spelling, information, and page placement. Once you are satisfied with the composition, print the text on the vellum.

❷ Glue the vellum to the cardstock along the right side of the papers. Make sure you align the left edge of the papers.

❸ Punch two holes in the left sides of the joined papers, about 1/4" from the left edge and 1/2" apart.

❹ Thread the ribbon through the holes and tie a loose knot. Angle off the ribbon ends.

❺ To make the envelope, using the 8-1/2" x 14" piece of cardstock, fold and crease both 14" sides in 1-3/8". Fold and crease one of the 5-1/2" sides up 5-3/4". Fold and crease the remaining paper down for the flap (should be about 2-1/2"). Cut excess paper from the flap so there is only one layer. Scallop the flap with decorative-edge scissors. Glue the sides of the folded envelope closed. To seal the envelope, use the glue stick.

Traditions

It is customary to send invitations six to eight weeks before the wedding.

Perfect Programs

Designed by
  Carolyn Vosburg Hall
Difficulty level:
  Easy (depending on
  computer skills)

YOU WILL NEED

Pre-printed 8-1/2" x 11" background papers for hand or
  computer text (Note that some papers have a barcode printed
  on the back)
Typing paper
Computer and printer
18" of ribbon (one piece per scroll)

❶ Type the text; carefully check spelling and grammar. Try
different formats, such as justified left, center balanced, two
columns, or justified on both sides. Try different fonts, including
a delicate script, a clear legible font, or an informal hand-letter-
ing style. Stick to one font style; you can vary the size for
emphasis. Print samples on typing paper to double-check
spelling, information, and page placement.
❷ Once you have created the page of text you want, hold it
behind the pre-printed background page for placement. (**Note:**
Holding the pages by a light source will make it easier to see.) If
it overlaps the background design or doesn't look right, redesign
the page by computer to fit. Repeat as often as necessary.
❸ Once you are satisfied with the look of your program, print a
sample copy. If it is okay, continue printing as many programs as
you need; if not, rework the design.
❹ Starting at the bottom end, roll the paper into a scroll about
1" across.
❺ Tie 18" ribbon around the rolled scroll and tie a bow.

TIP
Rather than just tie a bow around
the scrolls, try wrapping ribbon
around them in interesting ways
and add embellishments, like flowers,
to coordinate with the bouquets,
altar flowers, etc. Also, use a beautiful
basket for the scrolls to sit in;
why not decorate the basket, too?

*While standard folded programs
are very popular for a wedding
ceremony, why not create a scroll
instead? Make sure you provide all
of the ceremony information in the
right sequence—and that you spell
everyone's names correctly!*

Pastel Topiary, page 96

CHAPTER FOUR

The Reception

IN MEDIEVAL TIMES, wedding guests would return to the bride's family home for a feast after the ceremony. Since then, the reception has become a time for dancing and toasting the couple. The cake is served, the bouquet and garter are thrown, and the two families jovially intermingle to celebrate their union.

Before the guests even arrive, the reception hall is often ornately decorated with centerpieces, place settings, and place cards. Often the wedding theme is carried over, be that a common flower or a favorite color.

During the festivities, the symbolism of two families joining is played out through various dances. Long ago, the bride and groom would dance the first dance, and then the bride would dance with each man and the groom with each woman in attendance. In some families, it's common for the bride to dance with the groom's father and the groom to dance with the bride's mother.

Circle dances are also a common sight at weddings. In much the same way that wedding rings represent eternity, circle dances represent community. In Germany, married women would dance around the bride to welcome her. Whether or not the Hokey Pokey is a modern interpretation, we may never know!

The theme of sharing also threads itself through the reception. There are the cakes, the groom's fruit cake (which is now often made of chocolate) and the traditional white cake. The bride and groom cut the cake together, showing that they have become one; the guests share in the dessert and each takes home a piece of the groom's cake.

Starting in the sixteenth century, French royals began giving gifts, or favors, to their reception guests. While they would give gold, porcelain, and precious stones, as the custom caught on with lower levels of society, less expensive gifts like candy were common. Whatever the value of the gift, the message is always gratitude for sharing the splendid occasion.

IN THIS CHAPTER

Callas and Glass Centerpiece • 90
Callas Place Card Frame • 92
Callas Candle Holder • 92
Callas Favors • 93
Arched Centerpiece • 94
Pastel Topiary • 96
Favor Boxes • 98
Bubble Favors • 99
Cone Topiary • 100
Wedding Ring Centerpiece • 102
Swan Favors • 104
Bag Favor • 105
Box Favors • 106
Slipper Favors • 107
Decorated Toast Glasses • 108
Decorated Guestbook Pen • 109
Daisy Cake • 110
Terra Cotta Centerpiece • 112
Favor Boxes • 114
Chair Garland • 115
Rose Ivy Bowl • 116
Rose Place Card Holder • 117
Cherub Place Cards • 118
Wedding Bell Favors • 119

Callas and Glass Centerpiece

TIP

Make sure you have a reliable non-stick surface available for gluing the callas and leaves together.

Designed by Bucky Farnor
Difficulty level: Intermediate

YOU WILL NEED

6 medium-sized callas and accompanying leaves
12-1/2" tall glass vase
6" tall pillar candle, white
Hot glue gun and glue sticks
Wire snips

While this project looks easy to execute, it is somewhat tricky... but with its simple elegance it is worth the effort!

❶ You will be making two different callas and leaves arrangements. For the taller part, lay three callas on your work space, alternating their heights (the tallest calla should be about the same height as the vase): tallest on the left, shortest in the middle, and the "medium" on the right. Cut the stems flush and glue them together with a generous amount of glue.

❷ Glue three leaves—minus stems—to the front of the arrangement made in Step 1. When the glue is completely dry, flip the arrangement over and glue three leaves—with stems—to the back. Use the wire snips to make sure the bottom of the complete arrangement is flush.

❸ Manipulate the wires in the callas and leaves by bending them in different directions. Carefully glue the complete arrangement to the vase, with the bottom of the arrangement flush with the bottom of the vase. Use a generous amount of glue at the base of the arrangement and sparingly glue some of the stems to the vase.

❹ For the shorter part, lay one calla on the table and put a calla "head"—without the stem—on either side of it. Glue them together with a generous amount of glue.

❺ Glue three leaves to the front of the callas. Manipulate the wires in the callas and leaves by bending them in different directions.

❻ With a generous amount of glue, carefully glue the complete arrangement to the vase, to the left of the taller arrangement, with the bottom of the arrangement flush with the bottom of the vase. Sparingly use glue to attach some of the stems to the vase.

❼ Put the pillar candle into the vase.

Callas Place Card Frame

The white satin frame used for this place card is pretty enough to be used alone, but with the addition of callas and ribbon, it becomes a cherished keepsake.

Designed by Lisa Vollrath
Difficulty level: Easy

YOU WILL NEED

4" x 3" satin place card frame, white
Cardstock, white, in size to fit in frame opening
Pen or marker, black, or computer
3 callas with leaves intact
1 extra leaf
7" of 3/8" wide satin-edge ribbon, purple/blue
Hot glue gun and glue sticks
Wire snips

❶ Starting with the top-most calla glue the callas to the right side of the frame, in a linear fashion. Cut the stems flush with the bottom of the frame with the wire snips.
❷ Glue the extra leaf at the bottom of the frame, over the stems.
❸ With the ribbon, make a small bow. Glue the bow to the frame, just below the bottom calla.
❹ Either write the guest's name on the piece of cardstock or type it on the computer; slip into the back of the frame.

Callas Candle Holder

This candle holder is the perfect size to use as a centerpiece on guests' tables; it is large enough to be noticed, yet short enough so that guests' views will not be obstructed.

Designed by Lisa Vollrath
Difficulty level: Easy

YOU WILL NEED

3-1/2" tall x 3-1/2" wide glass
  candle holder (with lip)
Votive candle, white
2 callas and leaves
23" of 3/8" wide satin-edge
  ribbon, purple/blue
Hot glue gun and glue sticks
Floral tape
Floral wire
Scissors
Wire snips

❶ Cut 17" of ribbon; tie this piece around the candle votive so that it angles toward one of the upper corners. Tie a knot and secure with a dab of hot glue. Angle off the ribbon ends.
❷ With floral tape, secure two leaves to the two callas; the callas should be pointing in opposite directions.
❸ With the remaining 6" piece of ribbon and floral wire, make a small three-loop bow.

Secure the bow to the place where the callas and leaves are joined.
❹ Glue the callas ensemble to the knot of the ribbon tied around the votive in Step 1.
❺ Put the candle inside of the holder.

Miniature champagne glasses make ideal wedding favors. Here, tulle is used to keep the candy in place.

Designed by Lisa Vollrath
Difficulty level: Easy

YOU WILL NEED

Miniature plastic champagne glass
8" of 3/8" wide satin-edge ribbon, purple/blue
1 calla and leaf (Option 1 uses a small calla, while Option 2 uses a large calla)
1 8" diameter tulle circle
Hot glue gun and glue sticks
Scissors
3 candy kisses
Wire snips

Option 1
 Cut a hole in the bottom center of the tulle circle; make the circle large enough so that the tulle can be slipped over the bottom of the glass.
❷ Put the candy kisses into the glass.
❸ Gather the tulle and use the ribbon to secure the "pouch" with a bow. Angle off the ribbon ends.
❹ Glue the calla, without a stem, and leaf onto the bow's knot.

Option 2
❶ Cut a hole in the bottom center of the tulle circle; make the circle large enough so that the tulle can be slipped over the bottom of the glass.
❷ Put the candy kisses into the glass.
❸ Gather the tulle and use the wire stem of the calla and leaf to secure the tulle "pouch."
❹ Use the ribbon to tie a bow around the base of the tulle on the glass' stem. Angle off the ribbon ends.

Calla-trimmed Box Favor

White Jordan almonds look perfect in this clear plastic box!

Designed by Lisa Vollrath
Difficulty level: Easy

YOU WILL NEED

2" square plastic box
1 calla and leaf
9" of 3/8" wide satin-edge ribbon, purple
8" of 1" wide iridescent ribbon, white
Jordan almonds
Floral wire
Hot glue gun and glue sticks
Scissors
Wire snips

❶ Make a bow with the white ribbon. Glue the bow on the box, near the top. Angle off the ribbon ends.
❷ Glue the leaf to the bow's knot, with the leaf pointing toward the back of the box.
❸ Glue the calla to the end of the leaf, with the calla pointing toward the front of the box.
❹ Cut 8" of purple/blue ribbon. Use this length to make a bow. Angle off the ribbon ends.
❺ With floral wire, make a small loop with the remaining 1" of purple/blue ribbon. Secure this loop to the bow made in Step 4.
❻ Glue the bow and loop over the join of the leaf and calla.
❼ Fill the box with an odd number of Jordan almonds.

Arched Centerpiece

Designed by Bucky Farnor
Difficulty level: Advanced

YOU WILL NEED

For Taller Arrangement
8" tall vase, white
Floral foam, size to fit snugly in vase
2 5" tall Styrofoam hearts
1/2" wide satin ribbon, dark pink
5 feet of 1/2" wide satin ribbon, light pink
Bunches of hydrangea, pink iridescent
1 large rose, dark pink
2 rosebuds, dark pink
4 roses, light pink
4 stalks, white
Ivy
Geraniums
Eucalyptus, plum
Approximately 6 berry stalks, cranberry and white
Floral picks
Optional: Metal floral picks
Hot glue gun and glue sticks
Scissors
Wire snips

For Shorter Arrangement
8" tall vase, white
Floral foam, size to fit snugly in vase
5 feet of 1/2" wide satin ribbon, light pink
1 large rose, dark pink
2 rosebuds, dark pink
3 roses, light pink
2 stalks, white
Ivy
Geraniums
Eucalyptus, plum
Approximately 3 berry stalks, cranberry and white
Optional: Metal floral picks
Hot glue gun and glue sticks
Scissors
Wire snips

For Arch
About 8 stalks of eucalyptus, plum, each
   approximately 12" long
Ivy
Floral wire
Wire snips

Note: If you have difficulties inserting any of the components
into the floral foam, use metal floral picks.

The ultimate balancing act, this centerpiece features two separate arrangements joined by an arch of ivy and eucalyptus.

Taller Arrangement (left side)
❶ Put the floral foam into the vase; for extra stability, glue it in place.
❷ Cut the light pink ribbon into three pieces of varying lengths; tie all three pieces around the vase's neck. Tie knots in the ribbon ends.
❸ Glue one end of the dark pink ribbon to one of the Styrofoam hearts. Tightly wrap the ribbon around the heart; when finished, cut the ribbon and glue the end to the heart. Repeat for the other heart.
❹ Glue the iridescent hydrangea all around the ribbon-wrapped heart. Repeat for the other heart.
❺ Poke a floral pick into the bottom of one of the hearts. Repeat for the other heart.
❻ Rather than begin with the flowers, you will start with the taller elements: Insert white stalks and eucalyptus into the floral foam, near the back. The tallest element should be about 20" above the top of the vase.
❼ Start building downward, inserting two rosebuds and one pink rose into the foam, as well as the three remaining white stalks.
❽ Insert the large rose near the bottom of the arrangement, along with the remaining three pink roses, one on each side of the large rose and one to the left of the arrangement.
❾ Using both ivy and geraniums, fill in the arrangement, including the back. Use some pieces to create a cascading effect on the left side.
❿ Fill in the design with additional, shorter, pieces of eucalyptus, as well as the berry stalks.
⓫ Finally, insert the two ribbon-wrapped hearts into the arrangement.

Shorter Arrangement (right side)
For this arrangement, follow the instructions above for the taller arrangement, using fewer flowers, as described in the materials list. Here, the tallest item should be about 13" above the top of the vase, and there are no ribbon-wrapped hearts. Finally, make a cascading effect on the right side of the vase, which visually balances it with the taller arrangement.

Arch
❶ You will need about four pieces of eucalyptus for each side, which will be joined in the middle with floral wire. Set four pieces pointing upward on your workspace; place the other four pieces to the right, pointing upward. Using floral wire, join the eight pieces together so they are very secure.
❷ Intertwine ivy throughout the eucalyptus, using floral wire to secure if necessary.
❸ Bend the eucalyptus and ivy to form an arch.
❹ Insert the left side into the foam in the taller arrangement. Once it is completely secure, insert the right side into the foam in the shorter arrangement, moving the vase closer or farther from the taller arrangement.

Pastel Topiary

You can use any type of flower imaginable—in any pastel color—in this glorious topiary!

Designed by Bucky Farnor
Difficulty level: Intermediate

YOU WILL NEED

Various flowers, in any pastel color, including roses, hydrangea, and daisies
1 large rose, pink
1 sprig of ivy
8" tall container, brass
Floral foam, in size to fit into container
8" diameter Styrofoam ball
18" tall thick, heavy stem
Spanish moss
Floral wire
Wire snips

Note: It is easier to freeform this arrangement than give specific instructions; follow the basic look of the arrangement pictured.

1 Insert the floral foam into the container.

2 Insert the thick, heavy stem into the Styrofoam ball. Insert the other end into the floral foam.

3 Cut the stems off of the flowers, leaving about 3" intact. Surround the thick stem with the cut-off stems by sticking them into the floral foam.

4 Wrap floral wire around the stems near the Styrofoam ball to further secure.

5 Begin inserting the flowers into the ball; start at the top of the design and work your way around the ball and to the bottom, completely covering the place where the wire is securing the stems. Vary the heights of the flowers by clipping the stems to various lengths and pushing some further into the ball and others only slightly (yet enough to make sure they will stay inserted into the ball).

6 Cover the floral foam with Spanish moss, completely surrounding the stems.

7 Insert the large pink rose into the foam, at the front of the arrangement.

8 Insert the sprig of ivy into the foam, directly behind the rose.

Traditions

In Vietnam, both the bride and groom's families host a wedding party.

Decorated Favor Boxes

Designed by Lisa Vollrath
Difficulty level: Easy

The wonderful thing about these favor boxes is that they already are lined with tulle, so you just need to fill and decorate them.

❶ Fill the box with an odd number of Jordan almonds.
❷ Gather the tulle and, using the 1" wide ribbon, tie a bow. Angle off the ribbon ends.
❸ Cut the 3/8" wide ribbon in half. Using the two pieces of ribbon together and floral wire, make a multi-loop bow. Angle off the ribbon ends. Use the wire to secure the bow to the bow made in Step 2.
❹ Glue the bunch of flowers to the center point of the bows.

Floral Favor Boxes

Designed by Lisa Vollrath
Difficulty level: Easy

For this variation of the Decorated Favor Boxes, you will be adding color-coordinated hydrangea around the boxes.

❶ Hot glue hydrangea around the rim of the box, four on each side.
❷ Follow Steps 1 through 4 of the Decorated Favor Boxes above.

Traditions

It is customary to use odd numbers of candy for favors because they cannot be divided equally (symbolizing the bride and groom becoming one).

Tulle-wrapped Bubble Favors

Designed by Lisa Vollrath
Difficulty level: Easy

YOU WILL NEED

Bubble bottle and wand
Bubble solution (enough to fill the bottle)
2 hydrangea, both pink or 1 blue and 1 pink
1 10" diameter circle of tulle, white
1 foot of 3/8" wide satin ribbon, ivory, or 2 feet of 3/8"
    wide satin ribbon, pink
Hot glue gun and glue sticks
Scissors
Wire snips

Wrapped with tulle, these bottles of bubbles could easily be used as table favors rather than immediately after the ceremony.

❶ Fill the bottle with bubbles. Close the bottle with the wand.
❷ Glue one flower to the top of the wand. **Optional:** Before attaching the hydrangea, glue a leaf to the top of the wand.
❸ Enclose the bottle with the tulle circle.
Option 1: Cut the 2 feet of pink ribbon in half. Together, tie the two ribbons into a bow, around the bottle. Angle off the ribbon ends. Hot glue the remaining hydrangea over the bow.
Option 2: Cut the ivory ribbon in half. Together, tie the two ribbons into a knot, around the bottle. Angle off the ribbon ends. Hot glue the remaining hydrangea over the knot.

Flower-trimmed Bubble Favors

Designed by Lisa Vollrath
Difficulty level: Easy

YOU WILL NEED

Bubble bottle and wand
Bubble solution (enough to fill the bottle)
2 hydrangea, both pink or blue
1 foot or 2 feet of 3/8" wide satin ribbon, ivory
Hot glue gun and glue sticks
Scissors
Wire snips

This simpler version of the Tulle-wrapped Bubble Favors can be made quickly with minimal supplies.

❶ Fill the container with bubbles. Close the bottle with the wand.
❷ Glue one hydrangea to the top of wand.
Option 1: Cut the 1-foot long piece of ribbon in half. Together, tie the two ribbons into a knot, around the bottle. Angle off the ribbon ends. Glue the remaining hydrangea over the knot.
Option 2: Cut the 2-foot long piece of ribbon in half. Together, tie the two ribbons into a bow, around the bottle. Angle off the ribbon ends. Glue the remaining hydrangea over the bow.

Cone Topiary

Designed by Bucky Farnor
Difficulty level: Intermediate

YOU WILL NEED

3-1/2" tall by 4-1/2" wide brass pot
12" tall foam cone
1 yard of 2-1/2" wide satin ribbon, white
10 bunches hydrangea, white
10 large ivy leaves
1 package small dove charms, white
Bride and groom dove topper
Pearl-head pins
Hot glue gun and glue sticks
Scissors
Wire snips

For this centerpiece, charming white "love birds" are perched on a cone carefully wrapped with ribbon and hydrangea. To carry the bird theme throughout the piece, small plastic doves are inserted amongst the hydrangea.

1 Insert the foam cone into the container. For extra stability, glue it in place.
2 Insert the large ivy leaves into the base of the cone, where it meets the container; bend them downward.
3 Starting at the top of the cone, begin wrapping the ribbon downward, leaving spaces approximately 1" wide into which the hydrangea will be inserted. Secure the ribbon to the cone with pearl-head pins in any design you choose.
4 Fill in all of the spaces between the ribbon with the hydrangea.
5 Insert the dove charms into the cone, filling any gaps in the hydrangea.
6 Insert the bride and groom doves into the top of the cone.

Traditions

In Armenia, when a couple is married, two white doves are released which symbolize happiness and love.

Designed by Bucky Farnor
Difficulty level: Advanced

Wrapped in white satin ribbon, two Styrofoam circles are magically transformed into wedding rings that arch over and protect the bride and groom. Use an array of summery flowers and foliage to completely surround the couple with a lovely garden.

YOU WILL NEED

2 12" Styrofoam rings
10 yards of 2-1/2" wide satin ribbon, white
Fern fronds
Ivy bush
8" x 4" x 2" block of Styrofoam, white
5 large roses, white
12 rosebuds, white
2 ficus foliage sprays
9" wide x 4-1/2" tall bowl, white
2-1/2 yards of rose ribbon tulle, white
6" circles of tulle, white
3 sheer butterflies
6 stalks, white
Bride and groom statue
Optional: 12 small satin roses and 4 6" diameter circles
   of tulle
Pearl-head pins
White filler
Floral sticks
Floral wire
Hot glue gun and glue sticks
Scissors
Wire snips

Note: If you have difficulties inserting the flowers, foliage, or ribbon into the foam, use metal floral picks.

1. Put the Styrofoam block into the bowl.
2. Cut about a 2" section from one of the Styrofoam rings; cut another 2" section from the same ring, directly opposite the first cut section.
3. Starting with one of the cut sections of Styrofoam, glue the end of the ribbon to the end of the Styrofoam. Begin wrapping the ribbon around the piece, securing it with pearl-head pins. When you get to the end of the piece, cut off the excess ribbon and glue into place.
4. Cut three pieces of rose ribbon tulle, each approximately 16" long. Glue one section at a time to the ribbon-wrapped Styrofoam, one on each side and one on the outer edge.
5. Repeat Steps 3 and 4 for the other cut section, as well as the remaining 12" ring.
6. Insert one floral stick through the 12" ring, at the top and bottom. With the excess that is sticking out, attach the two Styrofoam sections.
7. To embellish the top of the joined rings, make a multi-loop bow from the satin ribbon and floral wire. Leave the ribbon ends about 6" and cut a "V" in them. Insert the bow into the top of the rings.
8. Fill in the area around the bow with various flowers and a little ivy.
9. To finish the top, insert the three butterflies at random.
10. Set the finished rings on the foam in the bowl. Use floral sticks to secure the rings to the foam.
Note: Now you will start filling the outer edges of the bowl with flowers and foliage. When you are designing, imagine you are creating four different designs, each divided by the four 2" wide rings.
11. Begin inserting the roses into the foam in the bowl; remember to reserve enough to use in all four sections.
12. After using all of the roses, insert white stalks and white fillers into the foam, again using them in all four sections.
13. Complete each section by filling them in with ferns and ivy. If desired, and there is any additional space, you can also use pieces of the satin ribbon, or multi-loop bows, to fill in gaps (use wire to secure the ribbon to the foam).
14. Set the statue in the middle of the rings.
Optional: Prior to setting the statue in the middle of the rings, you can embellish its base with small satin roses and tulle.

Swan and Tulle Favor

Dainty peach hydrangea are a pretty addition to this otherwise plain plastic swan.

Designed by Bucky Farnor
Difficulty level: Easy

YOU WILL NEED

Plastic swan
1 6" diameter tulle circle, white
6" of 3/8" sheer satin-edge ribbon, ivory
11 hydrangea, peach iridescent
Jordan almonds
Scissors
Wire snips

❶ Glue ten hydrangea around the front of the swan, five on each side of the neck.
❷ Put approximately seven Jordan almonds in the center of the tulle circle. Gather and secure with the ribbon; tie in a bow. Angle off the ribbon ends.
❸ Glue the remaining flower over the bow's knot. Put the tulle "pouch" into the swan.

Traditions

Sometimes candy is given in groups of five, a symbol of five wishes: fertility, health, happiness, love, and wealth.

Swan and Flower Favor

This pretty swan has a peony "hat" atop its head.

Designed by Bucky Farnor
Difficulty level: Easy

YOU WILL NEED

Plastic swan
1 24" x 6" piece of tulle, white
5 peonies with pearl sprays, ivory
Jordan almonds
Wire snips

❶ Glue one peony to the top of the swan's head, making it appear as a "hat."
❷ Glue the remaining four peonies to the back of the swan, with the stems inside of the swan.
❸ Put approximately seven Jordan almonds in the center of the tulle; tie a knot. Make a large bow with the tulle. Put the "pouch" into the swan.

Swan and Rose Favor

Designed by Bucky Farnor
Difficulty level: Easy

This favor is embellished with only tulle and a single rose. It is with this simplicity that it makes a statement.

YOU WILL NEED

Plastic swan
1 satin rose, white
2 6" diameter tulle circles, white
Jordan almonds
Floral wire
Hot glue gun and glue sticks
Scissors

1. Gather one piece of tulle in the center. Glue the center point to the inside back of the swan.
2. Glue the rose to the base of the tulle, inside the swan.
3. Put approximately seven Jordan almonds into the center of the remaining tulle circle. Secure the tulle "pouch" with floral wire. Cut off any excess tulle. Put the tulle pouch into the swan with the wire facing down.

Tulle and Ring Favor Bag

Designed by Lisa Vollrath
Difficulty level: Easy

Daisies and wedding bands dress up this simple favor bag.

YOU WILL NEED

Sheer favor bag
2 feet of 6" wide tulle, white
10" of 3/8" wide sheer satin-edge ribbon, ivory
2 wedding bands
2 daisies
Jordan almonds
Hot glue gun and glue sticks
Scissors

1. Put approximately seven Jordan almonds in the bag.
2. Wrap the piece of tulle around the bag; tie a knot.
3. Put the piece of ribbon over the tulle's knot; tie a bow with the tulle. Angle off the ribbon ends.
4. Two inches from each ribbon end, tie a wedding band with a knot.
5. Glue a daisy over each knot that holds the wedding bands.

Yellow-centered hydrangea add just the right amount of color to this traditional-looking favor box.

Designed by Lisa Vollrath
Difficulty level: Easy

YOU WILL NEED

Hexagon favor box, white
1 bunch hydrangea and berries, white
1/2 yard of 6" wide tulle, white
1 foot of rose ribbon garter tulle, white
Jordan almonds
Floral wire
Hot glue gun and glue sticks
Scissors
Wire snips

① Glue the rose ribbon garter tulle around the middle of the box.
② Fold the piece of tulle in half. Gather the center of the tulle and secure with floral wire. Glue the center point to the top of the box.
③ Glue the hydrangea and berries spray over the center point of the tulle.
④ Fill the box with an odd number of Jordan almonds.

Designed by Lisa Vollrath
Difficulty level: Easy

The daisies on this favor box add a light-hearted feeling.

YOU WILL NEED
Hexagon favor box, white
1 foot of 1" wide sheer satin ribbon, white, with embossed roses
1 paper rose, white
2 rosebuds, white
2 daisies
6" of 3/8" wide sheer satin ribbon, ivory
Jordan almonds
Hot glue gun and glue sticks
Scissors
Wire snips

① Glue the 1" wide ribbon to the box, around the middle. Cut off any excess ribbon, leaving just enough to overlap the end over the starting point. Where the ribbon overlaps, fold the edge and glue in place.
② Cut the 3/8" wide ribbon in half. Glue the two pieces to the top of the box, in an "X." Angle off the ribbon ends.
③ Glue the paper rose, two rosebuds, and two daisies to the top of the box, over the point where the ribbons cross.
④ Fill the box with an odd number of Jordan almonds.

Bow-trimmed Slipper Favor

Designed by Bucky Farnor
Difficulty level: Easy

Even Cinderella would be proud to have this pretty plastic slipper given at her reception!

YOU WILL NEED

Plastic slipper
1 foot of pearl trim
1 6" tulle circle, white
1 ribbon flower with pearls, white
Jordan almonds
Hot glue gun and glue sticks
Scissors

❶ Cut 3" off of the pearl trim (reserve for Step 3). Glue the remaining 9" strand around the slipper.
❷ Glue the flower to the slipper's "tip."
❸ Put approximately seven Jordan almonds in the center of the tulle. Gather and secure with the 3" of pearls. Put into the slipper.

Flower-trimmed Slipper Favor

Designed by Bucky Farnor
Difficulty level: Easy

With their light, fresh look, white hydrangea are the perfect complement to this slipper favor.

YOU WILL NEED

Plastic slipper
1 6" diameter circle of tulle, white
11 hydrangea, white
Jordan almonds
Floral wire
Hot glue gun and glue sticks
Wire snips

❶ Glue two hydrangea to the back of the slipper, at the top.
❷ Glue the remaining nine hydrangea around the front of the slipper, one at the "tip" and four on each side.
❸ Put approximately seven Jordan almonds in the center of the tulle. Gather and secure with a small piece of floral wire. Put into the slipper.

Designed by Lisa Vollrath
Difficulty level: Easy

YOU WILL NEED

Bride and Groom champagne glass set
2 paper roses, ivory
2 yards of 3/8" wide sheer stripe ribbon, ivory
Scissors

Typically, the best man has the honor of giving the first toast to the newly married couple. Here, the bride and groom can enjoy that toast with glasses that can easily be coordinated with the rest of the reception pieces.

❶ Cut the ribbon into three 12" lengths; cut one piece in half to make two 6" lengths.
❷ Using floral wire and one 12" piece of ribbon, make a multi-loop bow. Cut off the excess wire. Angle off the ribbon ends.
❸ Tie one 6" piece of ribbon in a knot around the glass' stem. Angle off the ribbon ends.
❹ Glue the bow from Step 2 over the ribbon knot made in Step 3.
❺ Glue a rose to the center of the bow, over the wire.
❻ Repeat Steps 2 through 5 for the other glass.

In Poland, if the bride drinks a glass of wine at the reception without spilling even a drop, she will have good luck. In France, the bride and groom drink from a two-handled cup that will be passed on to their children.

Traditions

Decorated Guestbook Pen

Designed by Lisa Vollrath
Difficulty level: Easy

YOU WILL NEED

1 ranunculus spray
3/8" wide sheer stripe ribbon, white
Floral tape
Floral wire
Pen and base, white

This decorated pen can be made in three very easy steps. For a coordinating set, you could also embellish the cake service set with the same flowers and ribbon.

1. With floral tape, secure the three ranunculus together, adding four leaves.
2. Using floral wire and ribbon, make a multi-loop bow. Using the wire to secure, join the bow to the roses and leaves.
3. Slide the ensemble over the bottom of the pen so that it rests on the base.

Traditions

Today, while guests often sign a guestbook at the reception site, in olden days, all who witnessed the wedding signed immediately following the wedding ceremony.

Daisy Cake

Designed by Wilton Industries
Difficulty level: Intermediate

Serves 57. **Note:** The top tier is often saved for the first anniversary. The number of servings given does not include the top tier.

YOU WILL NEED

8", 10", and 12" round x 3" high pans
3, 16, and 102 tips
Color, Lemon Yellow
Petite Double Rings ornament
Buttercream frosting
Royal icing
Flower Nail No. 7
1 14" Round Separator Plate
Flower Former Set
Wooden Dowel Rods
Meringue Powder
Cake boards
Waxed paper
Granulated sugar
Plastic bag
Optional: 3" Grecian Pillars and fresh flowers

1 Tint the sugar in advance: Place the desired amount of granulated sugar in the plastic bag and add small amounts of icing color to the bag. Knead until the color is evenly distributed throughout sugar. Sprinkle sugar on waxed paper to dry. Set aside.

2 In advance, using Royal icing and the flower nail, make approximately 130 tip 102 daisies with tip 3 dot centers. Sprinkle flower centers immediately with colored sugar and let 65 flowers dry flat and the remaining 65 flowers dry on flower formers.

3 Ice each one-layer cake smooth and prepare for stacked and pillar construction. Add a tip 16 shell bottom border on all cakes. Position the flowers and ornament.

4 **Optional:** You can put the cake on top of the Grecian pillars and fill in the bottom area with fresh flowers, if desired.

Daisies, which have come to symbolize both love and innocence, are featured in this cheery, summery cake.

Dot the center of the flower nail with icing; this will serve as a guide. Starting at any point near the nail's outer edge, squeeze and move the tip toward the icing dot. Stop pressure and pull the tip away. Repeat for a total of twelve petals. Add the flower center, press to flatten, and sprinkle with colored sugar.

Traditions

In ancient times, wedding cakes were made of wheat to symbolize fertility.

Terra cotta and a grapevine wreath match perfectly with the colors of autumn's bounty, including orange, yellow, and purple.

Designed by Bucky Farnor
Difficulty level: Intermediate

YOU WILL NEED

6" tall terra cotta pot
2 8-1/4" diameter terra cotta plates
13" diameter grapevine wreath
9" tall x 3" wide rectangular candle, orange
2 2" square blocks of floral foam
River stones, brown
3 apples, 2 red/yellow and 1 green
10 zinnias, yellow and yellow/orange
4 bunches grapes
Leaves, in fall colors
Approximately 10 stalks of bittersweet
Floral picks
Hot glue gun and glue sticks
Wire snips

❶ Glue one piece of floral foam to the wreath. Glue the other piece to the wreath, directly across from the first piece.
❷ Turn one terra cotta plate over so the bottom is facing up. Slip the wreath over this plate.
❸ Glue the other terra cotta plate, facing up, to the other.
   Note: You will be creating the design around the two pieces of floral foam so that there are approximate 6" gaps between the two sides.
      ❹ Put one floral pick into each apple. Insert the apples into the floral foam, one on one side, two on the other.
❺ Insert the zinnias into the floral foam, five on each side.
❻ Using about five stems on each side, glue the bittersweet to the wreath. Glue the stems so that they are pointing in different directions, adding height and length to the design.
❼ Glue two bunches of grapes to one side of the wreath, one on each side of the floral foam. Repeat for the other side.
❽ Fill in each side of the design with leaves, extending the design below the floral foam and around the grape bunches.
❾ Turn the terra cotta pot over so the bottom is facing up. Set the terra cotta plates and wreath on top of the terra cotta pot.
❿ Put the candle in the middle of the plate.
⓫ Fill in the area around the candle with river stones.

Traditions

Following a wedding ceremony in Croatia, all in attendance walk around a well three times, which symbolizes the Holy Trinity, as well as throw apples into it, as a wish for fertility.

Round Favor Box

Designed by Lisa Vollrath
Difficulty level: Easy

Orange handmade paper is the perfect background for this fall-inspired favor box.

YOU WILL NEED

3" diameter (round) corrugated box

Handmade paper, orange, in
size to cover the box lid

2 4" strands of raffia,
burgundy

3 sunflowers

2 rosebuds, red

1 rosebud, yellow

Bittersweet

Tacky glue

Hot glue gun and glue sticks

Candy

Scissors

❶ Put tacky glue on the top and sides of the box lid. Centering the paper over the top of the lid, smooth the paper over the lid and around the sides.

❷ Cut small slits in the paper to help it curve around the inner lid. Put tacky glue on the inside of the lid and smooth the paper over the glue.

❸ Tie the raffia together, in a knot. Hot glue the knot to the lid, toward one edge. Pull the raffia strands to make them appear fuller.

❹ Hot glue the two red rose-buds, one yellow rosebud, and the bittersweet to the lid, over the raffia knot.

❺ Hot glue one sunflower behind the two large roses and the remaining two sunflowers to a raffia strand, one on each side of the arrangement.

❻ Fill the box with an odd number of candies.

TIP

Why not make each of these favor boxes and alternate them at the place settings? You can fill them with such non-traditional candies as candy corn or peanut butter kisses to continue the fall feeling.

Square Favor Box

Designed by Lisa Vollrath
Difficulty level: Easy

If you love sunflowers, this pretty favor box is for you!

YOU WILL NEED

2-1/2" square corrugated box

Handmade paper, orange, in
size to cover the box lid

2 4" strands of raffia,
burgundy

16 sunflowers

2 rosebuds, red

1 rosebud, yellow

Bittersweet

Tacky glue

Hot glue gun and glue sticks

Candy

Scissors

❶ Put tacky glue on the top and sides of the box lid. Centering the paper over the top of the lid, smooth the paper over the lid and around the sides.

❷ Cut small slits in the paper to help it curve around the inner lid. Put tacky glue on the inside of the lid and smooth the paper over the glue.

❸ Hot glue four sunflowers to each side of the lid.

❹ Tie the raffia together, in a knot. Hot glue the knot to the center of the lid. Pull the raffia strands to make them appear fuller.

❺ Hot glue two red roses, one yellow rose, and the bitter-sweet to the lid, over the raffia knot.

❻ Fill the box with an odd number of candies.

Chair Garland

With its joined grapevine circles, this chair garland brings a feeling of the outdoors in. Depending upon the type of chair you are using, you can either add a fitted covering or piece of fabric over the chair back or leave it without, as shown here.

Designed by Lisa Vollrath
Difficulty level: Intermediate

YOU WILL NEED

5 3" diameter grapevine circles
6 small paper rosebuds, yellow
12 small paper roses, red
6 groups of 3 small sunflowers,
   with 3 leaves
10 sprigs eucalyptus, plum
Bunch of raffia, cranberry (you will
   need approximately four 16"
   lengths to join the circles and
   enough to connect the ends
   around the chair)
Hot glue gun and glue sticks
Measuring tape
Scissors
Wire snips

❶ Cut 16" lengths of raffia. Join the five grapevine circles with approximately four strands of raffia between each; tie in a bow. Pull the strands apart to make them appear fuller.

❷ Measure the chair's back, all the way around. For the end pieces, tie a bow but leave the outer raffia lengths long enough to tie around the chair in a knot or bow. Pull the raffia strands apart to make them appear fuller.

❸ Glue two small sprigs of eucalyptus, pointing downward, to the center point of each bow.

❹ Spreading the three leaves apart, glue one bunch of sunflowers over the eucalyptus sprigs, again pointing downward; the center point of the three leaves will be attached to the center point of the bow.

❺ At the join of the bow, eucalyptus, and sunflowers, glue one yellow rosebud and one red rose on each side of it.

❻ Tie around the chair.

Rose Ivy Bowl

Designed by Bucky Farnor
Difficulty level: Easy

This charming centerpiece uses the basic idea of the Rosebud Halo on page 69, except this version uses more flowers and rosebuds for a fuller appearance.

❶ For the "halo," you need two equal length sections to be joined in an approximate 13" circle. To make each section, using floral tape, join roses and white flowers, alternating one white flower with about three roses. Repeat this procedure for both sections.

❷ Join the two sections with floral wire, bending the sections to form a circle.

❸ Glue one end of the pearl strand to the rim of the ivy bowl. Wrap the strand around the bowl as many times as you can. Glue the end of the pearl strand to the wrapped section.

❹ Glue six white flowers to the rim of the bowl, with the first covering the end of the strand glued in Step 3. Space the six flowers equally around the bowl.

❺ Put the candle in the bowl.

❻ Set the bowl in the circle made in Step 2.

Rose Place Card Holder

Designed by Bucky Farnor
Difficulty level: Easy

*The word "topiary" means cutting or trim-
ming trees or shrubs into odd or ornamental
shapes. Here, you will be using roses and
floral tape, rather than scissors, to create a
round shape that could easily be used as a
centerpiece if not a place card holder.*

YOU WILL NEED

Approximately 60 roses, red
22" sheer satin ribbon, red
Brass container, 3" tall x 2-1/2" wide at top
Floral foam, in size to fit into container
Spanish moss
3-1/4" x 3" piece of cardstock
Marker or calligraphy pen, black
Sturdy round stick
Floral tape
Scissors
Wire snips
Optional: Hot glue gun and glue sticks

❶ Using floral tape, join the roses together (reserving twelve to be used in Step 5) around one end of
the stick, forming a circle. Wrap tape along the
entire length of the stem.
❷ Tie a bow with the ribbon at the base of the
roses. Cut a "V" in the ribbon ends.
❸ Put the floral foam into the brass
container. Cover the top of the foam with
Spanish moss.
❹ Push the stick into the center of the
foam.
❺ Insert three roses into each corner of the container.
❻ Fold the cardstock in half, to make a card that is 3-1/4" x
1-1/2". Write the guest's name on the place card. Set the card on
the container. **Optional:** If the card does not stay in place, you can
glue it to the topiary stick.

Cherub Place Cards

Designed by Carolyn Vosburg Hall
Difficulty level: Easy (except for lettering, which takes skill)

YOU WILL NEED

Sheer ribbons (15" if putting through punched hole,
    22" if tying around card)
4-1/4" x 5-1/2" pieces of cardstock
Cherub stickers
Schaefer calligraphy pen set
Hole punch
Glue stick

A wide variety of stickers is available to decorate place cards in an instant, which is particularly helpful if you have many to make. You can achieve a different look by altering your letting style and using the ribbon in different ways.

For all cards, fold the cardstock in half to make a rectangle that is 4-1/4" x 2-3/4".

Ivory
Punch a hole in the upper left corner of the card, 1/2" from the corner. Place the cherub sticker below the ribbon on the left side of the card. Write the name on the remaining space. Use a 15" piece of ribbon and tie it in a bow, through the hole in the corner.

Red
Glue a strip of 1" x 4-1/4" cardstock in a contrasting color (white is shown here) onto the front of the folded card. Write the name on the strip. Place the cherub sticker over the left end of the white strip.

Gray
Place the cherub sticker on the right side and write the name on the left, near the top. Use a piece of 22" ribbon to tie horizontally around the card front. Tie a bow to finish.

TIP
The Schaefer calligraphy pen has three different nibs (pen points) of varying widths and four colors of ink cartridges, so you have lots of choices. The set also includes instructions on how to do Chancery lettering, showing how to draw a faint horizontal line for straight lettering and angled lines across it to keep the lettering tilt consistent. Draw these lines very lightly with a ruler and soft pencil, wait until the lettering ink dries, and use an art gum eraser to remove the lines. If you are not confident about lettering the cards by hand, you can also print them on a computer.

Wedding Bell Favors

Designed by Carolyn Vosburg Hall
Difficulty level: Bags easy, bells intermediate

YOU WILL NEED

6" x 14" pieces of white tulle (you will need two pieces
   for each bag)
Jordan almonds
17" pieces of assorted ribbon
ShrinkyDinks
Dove stamp by Cynthia Hart for Rubber Stampede, Inc.
Color Box Cat's Eye pigment brush pad, black
Permanent ink pen, black
Hole punch
Clear matte spray
Optional: glitter
Oven

These bags of candy serve both as a wedding favor and a keepsake for guests. The bag with candy is easy to assemble, but making the keepsake shrink bell is more complicated (the shiny sheet resists inks; water-soluble inks smear if you touch them and need to be sealed).

❶ Make a paper bell pattern that is 3" x 3" tall. Trace the bell on the ShrinkyDinks sheet and cut it out inside the lines. Punch a hole in the top (before baking!). Stamp the dove on the top of the bell. Write the bride's and groom's names and the wedding date with the permanent pen. Stay as neat as possible, with no smears. **Note:** Some inks and pens will not stick to this surface; read all the instructions on the product. While working, keep the surface clean.

❷ Bake the ShrinkyDinks, following the manufacturer's instructions, until it is reduced in size and flattens. Remove from the oven and mold to a slight curve. If the printing ink or pen is not waterproof, use a clear matte spray to stabilize it. Sprinkle and glue on some glitter, if you wish.

❸ Using 17" of ribbon, thread the ribbon through the bell and tie a knot.

❹ Place 13 coated almonds on the tulle; gather the tulle into a bag to contain them.

❺ Wrap the ribbon with bell around the tulle to make a bag, then wrap it to the front and tie a bow. **Optional:** If the first ribbon doesn't appear wide enough, tie another, wider, piece of ribbon around the bag.

Lawrence and Ariel Landers
and
Edward and Serena Jacobs
request the pleasure of your company
at the marriage of their children

Cynthia Joy
and
Kurt Edward

on Saturday, the 10th of February
in the year Two Thousand and One
at Three o'clock in the afternoon
St. John Bosco Mission
22618 Messina
Highland, California

Garden Reception to follow

Shadow Box, page 125

CHAPTER FIVE

After the Big Day

At the first weddings, there were no photographers and
no attendants making sure everyone signed the guestbook–
and the first brides probably didn't mail thank-you notes.
It's up to modern couples to create their own traditions when it comes
to preserving memories. Some couples place disposable cameras
on the reception dinner tables, so the guests are free to take candid shots
that can be a treasure trove of material for creating such
keepsakes as memory books.
Invitations can be immortalized on the surface of a candle.
Special frames can be made to house precious photos. Small decorations
from the wedding such as ribbons, bows, favors, or anything else
that the couple saved can make stunning additions to a
commemorative shadow box.
But, before the newly married couple should even consider preserving
their memories, there is one final special event to take part in: the
honeymoon! This retreat gives the newlyweds a
chance to push all of the wedding hustle and bustle out of their minds.
It was originally a time when the couple would go away for a month,
drink sweet alcoholic beverages and, hopefully, start a family.
While modern honeymoons seldom last a month, they are nonetheless a
time for the couple to reflect and look forward to their future together.

IN THIS CHAPTER

Callas Frame • 122
Photo Album Cover • 124
Shadow Box • 125
Winter Wedding Scrapbook Page • 126
Our Wedding Day Scrapbook Page • 126
Thank You Card •127

Callas Frame

Designed by Betty Auth
Difficulty level: Intermediate

This wooden frame is made of pine, so it has hard and soft areas within the wood grain. This produces an interesting wood-burned line with lots of character, because the burning will be somewhat uneven. For that reason, it doesn't require experience to make it, and every project will be a little different from the next. Rubber stamps are a very easy method for placing the design on the wood, and the tiny clay flowers repeat the calla lily theme across the base of the frame.

YOU WILL NEED

Walnut Hollow Rectangle Frame, 12-1/2" x 11", with a 5-1/2" x 7" opening
Walnut Hollow Creative Woodburner
Walnut Hollow Mini Flow Point
Walnut Hollow Cone Point
Sandpaper, medium and fine grits
Plastic eraser, white
Rubber Stampede small Calla Lily rubber stamp
Fabrico Water-based Fabric Ink Pad by Tsukineko, Poppy Red*
1 package Modern Romance Clay Calla Lilies, white
Wire cutters
Delta Gel Blending Medium
Delta Ceramcoat Acrylic Paint, Autumn Brown or Fruitwood Gel Stain
Delta Ceramcoat Acrylic Paint, Mello Yellow
Delta SoftTints, White and Leaf Green
Delta Matte Interior/Exterior Water-based Varnish
Delta Sobo White Glue or hot glue gun and glue sticks
1/2 yard of 1/4" wide satin ribbon, white
Lint-free rag
Flat, soft bristle paintbrush
Small, round paintbrush
Masking tape

*Use an ink color for wood burning because black may run and brown will make it difficult to see where you have already burned.

1. Sand the frame with the wood grain and round off the sharp edges, beginning with medium grit sandpaper and finishing with fine.
2. With the rubber stamp and red ink, stamp four images evenly down each side of the frame and space two images equally across the top. Leave the bottom of the frame clear for adding the flowers.
3. With the Mini Flow Point, burn over the stamped outlines, burning the smaller details with the Cone Point.
4. Stain all surfaces of the frame, wiping off most of the stain. Paint the stain on the wood, working with a small section at a time, then blot well with the lint-free rag to avoid smearing and rub off most of the color. Use this method for staining the brown areas and also for the flowers and leaves (see Step 5). Allow to dry.
5. Use the White SoftTints to stain the calla lilies and the Leaf Green to stain the leaves.
6. With the small brush, paint the flower stamens Mello Yellow, but don't rub off as you did for the stain. Should you get some SoftTints color on the background when you wipe the stains, use the white eraser to remove it.
7. If necessary, go back over some of the wood-burned lines with the burner to darken them again.
8. Varnish all surfaces of the frame with Matte Varnish, let dry, and add another coat. Do not wood burn again once you have applied the varnish.
9. Leave the clay flowers in a bundle and cut the stems down to about an inch below the leaves. Fan them out and glue to the front of the frame, as shown.
10. Slip one end of the ribbon under the flower stems and tie tightly. Curl and twist the ribbon randomly on each side of the clay flowers and glue to the frame with tiny dots of glue.

TIP
Wood burning: Before beginning, tape the wire holder to the work surface so it won't slip around. Insert the Mini Flow Point in the burner and tighten well. Plug in the wood burner and heat for about five minutes. Never touch the metal parts of the burner and always unplug it when not in use. Change points only with rubber- or plastic-handled pliers. The darkness of the burn is controlled by the length of time the point rests on the wood, so there is no reason to push the point down into the surface. Work very slowly, and let it flow over the wood. When you begin or end a line, lift the point so it does not continue to burn. Work in a well-ventilated area to avoid breathing the fumes if you are sensitive to them. You can use a small fan to blow the smoke away, but have it directed across the project and not onto the wood burner, or it will cool too much to burn well.

TIP
You can use a color photograph, or have one printed in black and white to create a "heritage" look.

Photo Album Cover

Designed by Blanche Lind
Difficulty level: Easy

YOU WILL NEED

Memory album, white
Craft foam, white
1 sheet Grafix Double Tack Film
1 yard cord, gold
Tiny glass marble beads
Iridescent glitter
Photos of the bride and groom
Scissors
Pencil
Paintbrush
Large box or lid

It doesn't take much to make an otherwise plain photo album cover into a beautiful, personalized keepsake!

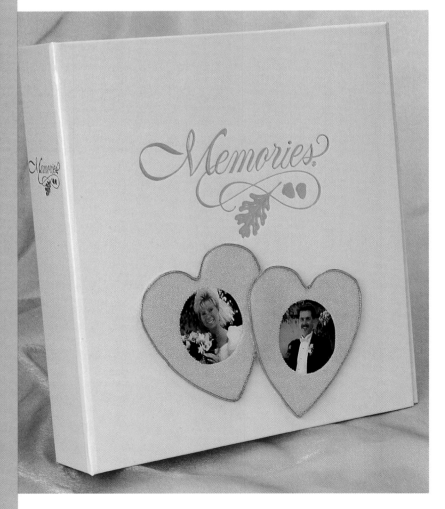

❶ Trace the heart pattern on the craft foam twice. Cut out the hearts.
❷ Peel one side of Tack Film and lay the hearts on the exposed sticky side. Allow sufficient room to fold the film over the hearts so that both sides are covered. Trim around the hearts.
❸ Peel the backing from one side of one heart and position on the album. Peel the film backing off the heart. Repeat for the second heart, overlapping the first slightly.
❹ Place the gold cord around the hearts, making sure it is secured to the film. Cut any excess.
❺ Cut out the photos of the bride and groom, in any shape desired, and center one on each heart.
❻ Place the album in the large box or lid. Pour the glass marble beads over the hearts, pressing firmly. Pour off any remaining beads and save.
❼ Sprinkle iridescent glitter over the hearts. Brush off any excess beads and glitter with the paintbrush.

HEART PATTERN
Enlarge 200%, then
cut two from craft foam

Shadow Box

Designed by Blanche Lind
Difficulty level: Intermediate

Preserve your wedding invitation with style! Clear crystal glass beads and glitter add sparkle and shine in this classy presentation. Instructions for the invitation shown are on page 86.

YOU WILL NEED

8" x 10" x 1-1/2" display case
Cardstock, purple, in pieces to cover all inside surfaces of display case
Invitation
2 appliqués
2 wedding bands
2 sheets Grafix Double Tack Film
Clear crystal glass beads
6 medium and 6 small silk flowers and leaves
1 dove
3" sheer 1" wide ribbon, lilac
Iridescent glitter
Glue stick
Scissors
Paintbrush
Large box or lid

❶ Take the inside portion (the shadow box) of the display case out of the frame. Glue the purple cardstock to all of the inside surfaces of the shadow box.

❷ Peel one side of 8" x 10" protective covering of double-faced Tack Film and place it over the bottom piece of cardstock. Use the second piece of Tack Film to fit the four sides of the box. Peel off all of the protective covering.

❸ Position the wedding invitation in the center of the box.

❹ Place the box in the large box or lid. Pour the clear crystal glass beads in the box over the invitation, covering all surfaces (including the four sides). Press firmly. Pour out any remaining beads and save.

❺ Sprinkle the iridescent glitter over the glass beads. Brush off any excess beads and glitter with the paintbrush.

❻ Glue the lace appliqués in the upper corners of the box.

❼ Tie the wedding bands together in a knot with the ribbon. Angle off the ribbon ends. Glue the knotted ribbon to the box, between the appliqués.

❽ Arrange and glue the silk flowers in the bottom corners of the box. Glue the dove in one of the corners.

❾ Put the box back into the frame.

Winter Wedding Scrapbook Page

Designed by Amy Gustafson for Hot Off The Press
Difficulty level: Easy

A red, gold, and green color combination is accented with snowflake vellum for a sophisticated holiday wedding page.

YOU WILL NEED

Patterned Paper Pizazz™, red moiré (Black & White Photos)
Specialty Paper Pizazz™, vellum snowflakes (Vellum Papers), gold (Metallic Papers)
Solid Paper Pizazz™, green, black (Solid Jewel Tones)
Bell punch
Scissors

❶ Triple-mat the photo on gold, green, and black papers.
❷ Tear along one long side of the vellum sheet; place the strip along the left side of the page.
❸ Punch four bells from the gold paper and mat each bell on black. Cut four 1-1/4" squares from the green paper and mat each on black. Place the bells at alternating angles on the squares and space them evenly down the vellum strip.
❹ Place the photo on the upper right side of page. Print out (or write) journaling on white paper and trim it down to a 1-1/2" x 2-3/4" rectangle. Mat on black, then gold, then green, and then black again, and center it underneath the photo.

TIP
The vellum was attached to the page by placing the adhesive underneath the green squares.

Our Wedding Day Scrapbook Page

Vellum has so many possibilities! Here, designer Susan Cobb created a window effect by cutting an opening in the vellum to allow the background paper to show through. The window effect and the multiple photo mats place the focus of the page right where it belongs—on the photo!

Continued at top of next page

Designed by Susan Cobb
for Hot Off The Press
Difficulty level: Easy

YOU WILL NEED

Patterned Paper Pizazz™,
   hydrangeas, purple moiré
   (Very Pretty Papers)
Specialty Paper Pizazz™, metallic
   silver (Metallic Papers), vellum
   lace border (Vellum Papers,
   also by the sheet)
Solid Paper Pizazz™, muted
   lavender, muted blue lavender
   (Solid Muted Colors), cream
   (Plain Pastels)
14" of 5/8" wide satin ribbon,
   lavender
Gel pen, silver
Pencil
Scissors

❶ Trim the hydrangeas paper to
an 11-3/8" square and glue to
the center of the purple moiré
paper. Multiple-mat the photo on
lavender, blue-lavender, cream,
and silver.
❷ Center the matted photo on
the vellum lace border sheet.
Using the dots as a guide, mark a
cutting line slightly larger than
the matted photo, about 1/4"
above and below the photo, and
1/8" at sides. Remove the photo
and cut out the marked rectangle.
❸ Glue the vellum lace border
sheet to the center of the
hydrangeas paper. Adhere the
photo to the hydrangeas paper
through the center of the vellum
opening. Journal on the vellum
with the silver pen.
❹ Tie a lavender ribbon and
glue to the lower left of the
photo, as shown.

Thank You Card

Designed by Susan Cobb
for Hot Off The Press
Difficulty level: Easy

*Express a sincere
"thank you" to the
special people who
helped make your day
just perfect! This card
is versatile enough to
be sent to a brides-
maid, parent, wedding coordinator—or anyone else who
helped make your wedding a beautiful occasion.*

YOU WILL NEED

5" x 6" Paper Flair™ blank card, ivory
Paper Flair™ Blossoms & Buds Paper Pack, Vellum Paper
   Pack
Heart motif: Paper Flair Laser Motifs Card Embellish-
   ments
Gel pen, gold
X-acto knife, cutting mat
Ruler

❶ Cover card front with gold paper. Cut a 4-1/2" x 6" piece of vellum
heart paper and glue to the center of the gold paper. Cut a 3-1/2" x 5"
piece of white roses paper and glue to the center of the vellum piece.
❷ Cut out the heart laser motif and trim the straight edges to a 1/8"
border. Place the laser motif in the upper center of the rose paper and
trace around the inside rectangle of the laser design with a pencil.
Remove the laser motif and open the card onto a cutting surface. With
the X-acto knife and ruler, cut out the penciled rectangle from the card
front only.
❸ Mat the heart laser motif on gold paper, trimming the edge to a
1/8" border. Glue to the inside back of the card, making sure the laser
heart is centered through the front window.
❹ Write "Thank You" below the window on the card front with the
gold pen.

Project Index by Theme

GENERAL

Bead Strung Jewelry Set.........................72
Bottle Centerpiece 19
Cherub Place Cards 118
Hat Place Card......................................17
Layered Invitation 86
Our Wedding Day Scrapbook Page 126
Perfect Programs 87
Photo Album Cover 124
Roses and Hearts Shower Cake 20
Shadow Box...125
Suede Jewelry Pouch 70
Thank You Card 127
Tiered Ivy Bowl Centerpiece...................17
Wedding Bell Favors 119
Whimsical Centerpiece...........................18
Whimsical Favors and Photo Album........16

CALLAS

Callas and Berries Arm Sheaf 26
Callas and Berries Nosegay 28
Callas and Glass Centerpiece 90
Callas and Pearl Comb...........................31
Callas and Satin Arm Sheaf 24
Callas Boutonniere 30
Callas Candle Holder 92
Callas Favors 93
Callas Frame 122
Callas Place Card Frame........................92
Callas-trimmed Bag 30

SPRING

Arched Centerpiece 94
Bubble Favors 99
Favor Boxes 98
Hand-wrapped Bouquet 34
Heart Pew Bow 77
Hydrangea Boutonniere 40
Lily and Hydrangea Nosegay 32
Lily Corsage 40
Pastel Topiary..96
Periwinkle Scabiosa Cone......................36
Ribbon and Hydrangea-trimmed Veil......41
Ribbon and Rose Hair Bow 42
Rosebud Ring Pillow 43
Satin Flower Girl Basket 38
Unity Candle Holder 76

SUMMER

Bag Favor 105
Box Favors 106
Braided Pew Box 83
Bridal Garters 57
Cone Topiary 100
Daisy Cake..110
Decorated Guestbook Pen 109
Decorated Toast Glasses 108
Double Orchid Corsage 52
Garden Altar Arrangement......................80
Gardenia and Ribbon Bouquet...............46
Mixed Cascade Bouquet 50
Orchid Cascade Bouquet 48
Pearl and Satin Comb 55
Pearl and Satin Veil 54
Ranunculus Pew Bow..............................82
Rose Arm Sheaf 44
Single Orchid Corsage 52
Single Rosebud Boutonniere 53
Slipper Favors 107
Swan Favors 104
Trimmed Ring Pillow 56
Triple Rose Corsage 53
Unity Candle Set 78
Wedding Ring Centerpiece 102

AUTUMN

Attendant's Basket 62
Cascading Bouquet 60
Chair Garland 115
Fall Harvest Altar Arrangement 84
Favor Boxes 114
Raffia-wrapped Bouquet 58
Terra Cotta Centerpiece 112

WINTER

Gardenia and Rose Bouquet 64
Red Rose Bouquet 66
Red Rose Clutch 67
Ribbon and Rose Ball 68
Rose Ivy Bowl 116
Rose Place Card Holder 117
Rosebud Halo 69
Winter Wedding Scrapbook Page 126